Praise for the First Edition of *Baby Bust*

T0031642

"What a wonderful book. Stew Friedman stands out as one of the few male voices in the field. He understands better than anyone else how leadership, life, and business can fit together. *Baby Bust* offers a fascinating glimpse into how young people think about their work, their families, and their futures. It's a succinct and invaluable read for managers, politicians, and all men and women seeking to better understand how the world is changing and to support greater freedom of choice."
—**Anne-Marie Slaughter, President and CEO,**
New America Foundation

"Provocative and practical, Stew Friedman's *Baby Bust* draws on his landmark study to document the metamorphosis in men's and women's views and expectations for work and family. As more women are leaning in to their careers, more men today want to be actively engaged in fatherhood. But both see conflicts between work and family life that are increasingly keeping them from choosing to be parents. Revelatory and rigorous, this urgent call to action is required reading for anyone who wants both men and women to be able to choose the world they want to live in."
—**John Gerzema, Author, *The Athena Doctrine: How Women**
(and the Men Who Think Like Them) Will Rule the Future*

"Stew Friedman has always been a trailblazer, and he has done it again! The provocative finding that 2012 graduates of Wharton are much less likely to plan to have children than those 20 years ago will receive a great deal of attention. More importantly, Friedman has probed the complex reasons why, and these are even more significant and telling. A must-read for everyone—employees, employers, and families—so that we can be much more intentional in creating the workplaces and family lives of the future."
—**Ellen Galinsky, President, Families and Work Institute,**
and Author, *Mind in the Making*

"Stew Friedman's unique cross-generational study finds both a triumphant new freedom for men and women and, at the same time, an indication of the deep conflicts between what we value and the lives to which we aspire. *Baby Bust* is a game-changing addition to the literature on work and family. Stew clearly and compassionately tells the story from the perspective of both men and women, echoing the challenges we all face as we seek to do meaningful work and have a meaningful life in today's frenetic and tumultuous world."
—**Brad Harrington, Executive Director,**
Boston College Center for Work and Family

"Important data and fascinating insights about the revolution we are experiencing in work and family. A must-read for anyone seeking to better understand how the world is changing and what new models will require."
—**Leslie A. Perlow, Konosuke Matsushita Professor**
of Leadership, Harvard Business School,
and Author, *Sleeping with Your Smartphone*

"Stew Friedman's *Baby Bust* is a wake-up call for business. The lack of strong business and public support for the positive enactment of caregiving, breadwinning, and career advancement has redefined what employees see as possible in their lives. The future economic health and well-being of the U.S. may be at risk. This eye-opening study raises the critical questions and provides practical ideas for change."
—**Dr. Ellen Ernst Kossek, Basil S. Turner Professor of**
Management, Purdue University, Krannert School of
Management and President, Work and Family
Researchers Network

10TH ANNIVERSARY EDITION

BABY BUST

New Choices for Men and Women in Work and Family

STEWART D. FRIEDMAN

WHARTON
SCHOOL
PRESS
Philadelphia

Published by
Wharton School Press
An Imprint of University of Pennsylvania Press
Philadelphia, Pennsylvania 19104-4112
wsp.wharton.upenn.edu

Printed in the United States of America on acid-free paper

10 9 8 7 6 5 4 3 2 1

Ebook ISBN: 978-1-613-63-179-9
Paperback ISBN: 978-1-613-63-177-5
Hardcover ISBN: 978-1-613-63-178-2

With love to my beautiful babies, Gabriel, Harry, and Lody

Contents

Preface to the 10th Anniversary Edition

Ten years have passed since *Baby Bust* was first published. In the intervening years, much has changed. The generations I studied—Millennials and Gen Xers—have grown up, and another generation, Gen Z, has started to reach adulthood. We have experienced a pandemic. I have become a grandfather. What hasn't changed is the decline in the birth rate, fueled by greater choice for all genders in work and family, which I applaud, and by our failure to act—as a society, in our organizations, as individuals, and in our families—to make parenting more feasible, which is a great disappointment to me.

In this book, I document the reasons why so many Millennial men and women were planning to opt out of parenthood compared to their Gen X forebears, and I offer a set of recommendations for what can be done to reverse this trend and accelerate our societal commitment to children and families. In this anniversary edition, I am grateful for the opportunity to offer in this new preface a few observations about what has transpired over the past decade—and where we go from here.

One of the critiques of the book when it first appeared was that the findings, tracking two generational cohorts of students at the Wharton School, were not generalizable to other segments of society. But as it turns out, this privileged group, these people who had opportunities that others could not access—high-paying jobs, the ability to afford quality child care—were the canaries in the coal mine. If they could not see a way to make their careers *and* families work, how could those with fewer opportunities and resources square this circle?

Why Are Fewer People Having Children?

The birth rate had been declining in the years leading up to our 2012 study, and it has continued on this trend in the ten years since; estimates range from a lowering of 14 to 20 percent fewer births per woman in the United States between 2012 and 2022. As I describe in chapter 5, the broad trend of fewer young adults believing they can find a way to have careers and families is a threat to our long-term survival, even as it also represents greater freedom for people—especially women, but men too—to choose whether to become parents. To explain the decline in birth rates, researchers circa 2012 had pointed mainly to economic factors, such as economic insecurity following the late 2000s recession and the rising costs of housing, child care, health care, and student debt; to shifts in family life, especially increases in the ages of marriage and childbearing; and to the dissipation of pressures from outmoded norms that in earlier times inhibited women's labor force participation. Ten years later, there are additional headwinds through which we must cut.

In one of my recent MBA classes, students explored the many frightening effects of climate change. Then, in the following week, they read *Baby Bust* and discussed its implications for the world they were entering as future business leaders. One of the more heated discussions ensued after a student said, "Why would I bring a child into a world that's going to be uninhabitable?" This question was not nearly so present in the conversations I had with students and in organizations in 2013 and 2014, following the book's publication. Today, in addition to economic and social factors, young people are despairing about the literal future of the planet.

Prospective parents in the United States can see that there remains a disastrously low level of support for family leave and child care, making the choice to become a parent all the less feasible. It's true there has been progress in some municipalities and states for more beneficent family leave policy and, at all political levels, toward more affordable and accessible child care, thanks to the tireless efforts of grassroots activists in organizing for progressive social policy. But our nation continues to lag woefully behind on the world stage. In our current polarized cultural and political environment, the prospects for cooperative efforts toward stronger support for families with children are dimmer than they were ten years ago. Indeed, as I write, Congress just failed to allow the COVID-era child care funding allotments to continue despite clear evidence that this funding helped pull children out of poverty.

How the Pandemic Affected Our Choices

When this book was published, the world had not yet been jolted by the pandemic that began in 2020. When we entered lockdown, with nearly all white-collar professionals forced to work from home (many blue-collar employees were not so privileged), parents scrambled to try to act as ad hoc teachers. A great number of mothers and fathers realized for the first time how invaluable the services of professional educators are in not only teaching their children but minding them while parents devote their attention to work. At the same time, teachers in the United States today are under pressure to do more with less, and for less, while combating an ill-informed public that is aiming to handcuff—with irrational limits on such things as which books children can access and how children are allowed to refer to themselves—their ability to help students be prepared for the challenges of today and tomorrow.

The pandemic provided a natural experiment in how we organize the time and space requirements of our work, our family lives, and all our other social relationships. This inadvertently created more room for people to try new arrangements that enabled greater freedom and flexibility. Now, in the wake of this unanticipated explosion of innovation, tension and conflict abound as individuals and organizations struggle to apply what we've learned about flexible work against the backdrop of traditional notions of what work life should look like and how it has historically been conceived. Of course, work was certainly not always segmented from the home. Indeed, for most of human existence, whether in hunter-gatherer societies or farming communities, work and life coexisted in flexible and entwined ways.

Where Do We Go from Here?

The call to action described in this book is as relevant now as it was ten years ago, perhaps more so: We can create a world in which people are free to choose whether to become parents and to make the parenting path more feasible for those who want to pursue it. Having tried to be optimistic about the relationship between work and the rest of life since I began researching this area over three decades ago, I'm now more pessimistic about our ability to reverse the birth rate decline because the pace of change in providing a functional infrastructure of care has been and will likely continue to be slow. But my hope remains alive, kindled by the rapid growth of active and effective voices for change in all sectors of society, including in business organizations, which are responding to the demands of a new labor market intent on having positive social impact, voiced especially by working mothers and our youth.

In light of how our world has evolved over the past decade, I would prioritize two social policy recommendations I make in chapter 5: Provide world-class child care and make family leave available. And I would add a new recommendation: Value immigration as an effective means for keeping society vital through population growth and resist the impulse to repel immigrants. We need to vote for people in public office who will support these causes, who will create policy that provides real support for families and not simply offer "thoughts and prayers" and then talk about—but fail to act on—meeting the needs of children and those who care for them.

In organizations, more employers are experimenting with new models of employment that embrace the whole person in a way that supports commitment to both work and family. Indeed, another outgrowth of pandemic life was the visceral realization—as exposed on endless Zoom calls—that our coworkers had real and very important people and animals in their home environments; that our colleagues had significant priorities outside of work. We know there are methods to help individuals manage boundaries, reduce the negative spillover of work pressures on family life, make work more meaningful, enable flexibility, and enrich all parts of life by learning to lead in all of them. An increasing number of organizations are applying these models to good effect. They must because employees—parents *and* people who aren't raising children—are demanding them, especially now, in the wake of the pandemic. But the rate at which these changes in organizations are being made is plodding because resistance to them, rooted in tradition and short-term thinking, is hard to break through.

Family life is rapidly evolving, and there are many new sources of support available for parents to learn how to collaborate in raising children while pursuing work that brings them material comfort, reduced stress, and a sense of meaningful contribution to the world. My colleague Alyssa Westring and I offer one such model in *Parents Who Lead* (Harvard Business Review Press, 2020), and the field is proliferating to feed the hunger parents have for practical knowledge to inform the choices they face.

One source of my still-active hope for the future is the small but real progress we've seen on the exhortation in chapter 5 for men to lean in at home. The number of men actively striving toward a more egalitarian world is growing. To see fathers with babies sitting in the U.S. Congress is to see movement in the right direction. But the 2013 edition's observation that the matter of supporting children and parents is "not a women's issue, but a human issue" hasn't been embraced nearly enough by men in our stubbornly patriarchal society.

In sum, the hurdles we face toward becoming more genuinely committed to nurturing the next generation seem greater now compared to a decade ago, despite the progress we've made. Our

Wharton Work/Life Integration Project study described in this book offers a window into the hearts and minds of people in different generations as they contemplated their futures; a window that demographic studies don't provide because they don't have an interior view. I hope and expect you will find the story told by this research to be compelling, even ten years later, because its implications for how we can spur cultural change remain urgent if we are to secure a better future for our children and for theirs.

This is an idea about which I feel more deeply now that I've become a grandfather in the years since publication. Indeed, it keeps me up at night. One of the early pieces I published was a prologue to a special issue of *Human Resource Management* I edited on leadership succession in 1986. There I noted how Indigenous peoples were known to make major decisions "contingent upon the effects of the decision on seven generations hence." It's hard to imagine a compelling argument against such a criterion. But is unfettered capitalism capable of such wisdom?

Are you and I?

Stew Friedman
October 6, 2023

Introduction
The Game Has Changed

In October 1987, I became a father. My mind flooded with questions. In the very next class I taught, I brought some of those questions to my Wharton MBA students in our organizational behavior course: "What responsibility do you have as future business leaders to nurture the next generation of people in our society? If you choose to become parents, how will you manage to do so in a way that works for you, your family, your business, and your community?"

Hungry for knowledge, they replied with a question of their own: "You're the professor. Can you just tell us?" Thus began a conversation with students, colleagues, and thousands of people in public- and private-sector organizations around the world that I have been engaged in ever since.

The Baby Bust: New Choices and New Constraints

For me, tracking these issues has been the work of a professional lifetime. In 1991, I founded the Wharton Work/Life Integration Project at the Wharton School at the University of Pennsylvania. In one of our initiatives, we surveyed 496 members of the 1992 undergraduate class as they were departing, and established a baseline for our longitudinal study. Twenty years later, we repeated the survey for 307 members of the 2012 graduating class.

With few exceptions, members of the Wharton Classes of 1992 and 2012 aspired to be in long-term relationships. Roughly one-third of both cohorts were already in committed unions, and most of the rest expected to be headed that way. All told, 88 percent of the

Class of 1992, the Gen Xers, were in or planned to be in a permanent relationship. For the Class of 2012, the Millennials, the number was only slightly lower: 84 percent. "Permanent relationship," however, does not necessarily lead to "family," as we traditionally have understood this term. And here the differences between the two classes were staggering.

In our sample, the rate of college graduates who plan to have children has dropped by about half over the past 20 years. *In 1992, 78 percent said that they planned to have children. In 2012, 42 percent did.* And these percentages were nearly the same for men and women. Millennial men and women are opting out of parenthood in equal proportions.

Do you plan to have or adopt children?

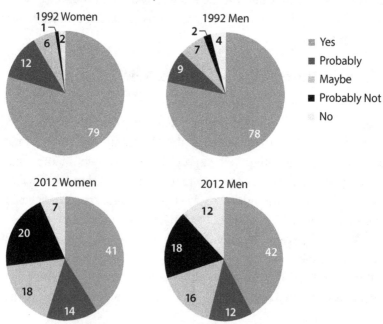

We are certainly not the first to observe a decline in birth rates, and this change in plans for children is not unique to young business professionals. It's part of a larger trend: a nationwide baby bust. Across the United States, births have dropped precipitously. In 1992 the average U.S. woman gave birth to 2.05 children over the course of her life. By 2007, this number had crept up slightly, to 2.12. But according to the Centers for Disease Control and Prevention, the average number of births per woman declined during each of the four years following 2007, dropping to 1.89 (preliminary estimate)— below the replacement rate of 2.10—in 2011.

The baby bust chronicled here has been even more dramatic. While the average 1992 graduate expected to have 2.5 children in his or her lifetime—well above the U.S. mean at the time—the average 2012 graduate planned to have only 1.7. But numbers can be deceiving, and these are so in one important way. Among those respondents in both 1992 and 2012 who planned to become parents, the number of expected children remained stable at 2.6. What caused the average of the expected number of children to plummet was the sharp decline in the portion of people who planned to have any children, through birth or adoption.

The baby bust, in short, is not about young people forming smaller nuclear families, that is, with fewer children. It is about the many who say they are simply opting out of parenthood altogether.

Many are writing about whether this is a good or bad thing for our society, and there are important arguments on both sides of the debate.[1] This book is instead about why both men and women are opting out of parenthood. And for men and women the reasons are quite different, signifying both new constraints and new possibilities.

I use our invaluable longitudinal data to tell the story of the baby bust and the radical changes that have occurred over these past two decades that have contributed to it. Most research on generational comparisons is cross-sectional, using information gathered in a snapshot from different age groups at one point in time; what's being compared in such studies are not necessarily differences between generations but differences between people of different ages, for example, 42-year-olds and 22-year-olds. Many such differences have nothing to do with social and cultural currents over time but everything to do with individuals being older. Our study design, which I'll describe, offers a unique vantage point because we asked questions of 22-year-old students as each class was graduating—first, the Class of 1992, and 20 years later, the Class of 2012.

Drawing on our evidence from these promising young business professionals from the Gen X and Millennial cohorts, I offer ideas about what we can all do now to brighten the prospects for our future vitality. I hope this book will inspire fresh insights for how you can play your part in the work/life revolution now under way.

The news is both bad and good. We found evidence of new challenges that are thwarting the family *and* career ambitions of young people today. Millennials foresee more intense conflicts between these two aspects of life. The time requirements of work have shot up astronomically (by 14 hours per week), and student debt has increased.[2] People are drowning in the deluge of data incessantly streaming at them.[3] Competition in the labor market has escalated, and we found that our Millennials feel pressure to conform to a narrow set of career paths. Being a parent is still very important for most young people, but many just don't see how they can manage it, so they are planning lives without children.

At the same time, we also observed greater freedom for men and women to choose paths that are meaningful to them, ones not prescribed by traditional expectations or narrowly defined gender role stereotypes. That is, for Millennials, being a man is no longer inextricably linked to being a breadwinning father, and being a woman is no longer synonymous with motherhood.

We also found that men and women are now more aligned about how to navigate *who* in a dual-career relationship should "lean in" to their careers and *when* they should do so. While some gender-stereotypical differences about family roles and dual-career relationships linger, today's young men *expect* to see women as peers in the workforce; they are more cognizant of the impending difficulties they, as men, will face in resolving conflicts between work and family life; and those young men thinking about having children see engaged fatherhood as a way of contributing to society. This is a gigantic leap forward for *man*kind, one that has positive repercussions for women and children. Millennial men are increasingly willing to experiment with new family and work models that enable both partners in a relationship to have more of what they want in life. Twenty years ago we saw a wide divergence between men and women on family role expectations; now there's more agreement about what it takes to make long-term relationships work, promising greater collaboration and mutual support.

A Different Conversation

The earthshaking resonance of Anne-Marie Slaughter's 2012 *Atlantic* article, "Why Women Still Can't Have It All," followed by the 2013 supernova that was Sheryl Sandberg's *Lean In* book-cum-social movement are compelling testimony to how much has changed. Back in 1987 it was strange for a man to be talking about work and family at a business school known mainly for its strength in finance. "Why," some of my colleagues wondered, "focus on this women's issue?" Thankfully, our new shared cultural understanding is that it's not a women's issue, but a human issue.

In addition to the continuing (albeit slow and insufficient) rise of women into positions of power, and more influential women speaking out and providing models for the new generation, men in positions of authority now recognize that they want something different for their children and are more inclined to try creative approaches. Further, given the increased desire that we and others have observed in young people to do work that matters and heals,[4] companies interested in competing successfully in the labor market are adjusting their brands as employers by emphasizing social impact, enhancing flexibility, and embracing diverse employee lifestyles.

We are all part of the work/life revolution now. Our collective failure to address adequately the issue of integrating work and the rest of life has *finally* emerged as the critical economic, social, political, and personal issue that it is, and it is deservedly capturing serious attention and accelerating experimentation with new models for work and family for men and women.

Everyone has an opinion because, for the first time, everyone has a stake and a voice. It affects you, whether you're a 60-year-old male CEO whose daughter is confronting the glass ceiling or whose son faces real constraints in his ability to figure out how he's going to fit your grandchildren into his life; a 25-year-old with no children who's managing a 45-year-old struggling to take care of his teenage children and aging parents; or single or married, gay or straight.

In Slaughter's *Atlantic* article we learned the story of a powerful woman with the courage to pull the curtain back and reveal the structural impediments to her being as available for her children as she wanted to be. It was a watershed event that tapped into the electrifying current of intergenerational differences, and it opened this discussion to a worldwide audience. Yet there had already been a body of evidence on what is needed and what works. Fifteen years ago, for example, our study of Wharton and Drexel[5] students resulted in a detailed 10-point action agenda (echoed in Slaughter's recommendations) that called for:

1. Reshaping the division of labor at home
2. Changing society's gender role ideology through education and socialization
3. Helping young people choose careers that fit their values
4. Teaching employees how to generate support from others
5. Investing in what employees do outside work

6. Creating work environments that value employees as whole people
7. Training managers to take a new look at work processes
8. Demonstrating the economic value of investing in family friendliness
9. Authorizing employees to think and act like entrepreneurs
10. Expanding childcare options, including through public-private partnerships

Of course, we were not the only ones advocating for such changes back then.[6]

As women (and some men) have worked for decades to help women enter and advance in the workforce, as women's presence in the workforce has grown so that a new generation of children has been raised by working parents, and as the changing (though not fully changed) division of labor at home strains *both* men and women, we have entered a new world. But our policies and organizational norms have not kept pace with these changing realities. Though there's been some progress, we still need more flexible career paths, better-quality child care, executives who recognize and respect the whole person, and more that I'll spell out in chapter 5.

Society is now ripe for more substantial change; there is at last the chance for long-known solutions to take root in fertile ground. We have reached a new level of collective awareness—which is good news for those who care about creating a more just society where men and women can participate in the spheres of work and home as they choose.

If 20 years after we first asked graduates about "having it all" many are now saying that they are opting out of parenthood, downsizing their family ambitions, why should we be cautiously hopeful? Because we are finally discussing openly the elephant in the room: the world has changed, but our institutions have not. The level of frustration has increased to the point where there is now the critical mass of interest required for propelling real progress. What is heartening about this moment is how many have joined the conversation. This will undoubtedly increase the options available for our companies, our families, our communities, and our selves. We've reached a tipping point, so there are grounds for optimism, even if the path ahead is fraught with significant obstacles.

About Our Sample and Methods

Our study design allows us to explore differences between two large samples of students from one of the world's leading business schools—privileged, ambitious, and highly talented young entrants to the professional labor market. One of the benefits of studying this group is that if *they* are having difficulty navigating the chaotic and increasingly fluid world of work, family, and society, then we can see our results as conservative estimates of the obstacles facing those who don't have access to the same resources—which is, of course, most people. However, this is a distinctive slice of American culture, so generalizations from our results must be made cautiously. Still, presumably these young people will be part of the leadership in our society to come, so these data provide a useful window into how the next generation envisions its future.

There are some important differences between the two cohorts in our study. The Class of 2012 was more likely to be female, international, and nonwhite, with proportionally more Hispanics and Asians. It was also wealthier and more left-leaning politically.

The curriculum at Wharton changed somewhat during this time, too. But the fact that all were selected for, and completed, this program gives us a powerful and relatively rare means for contrasting these two generations. We have survey data from two points in time 20 years apart, so we are able to see generational differences without having to worry about the effects of individuals' aging, with retrospective recollections colored by all that has intervened.

Because of changes in society over these two decades, members of the Class of 1992 and those of the Class of 2012 grew up not only in different generations, but also in different families. Graduates in 2012 were more likely to grow up with a working mother. This difference reflects nationwide trends in maternal employment.[7] Compared to 20 years ago, far more of today's young people grew up in either dual-career households or households with female breadwinners. Parents of the Millennials in our sample were better educated, too. In 1992, 45 percent of respondents' fathers and 22 percent of respondents' mothers had earned a graduate or professional degree; this compares to figures of 58 percent and 47 percent, respectively, in 2012. No doubt these dissimilar family experiences (at least in part) helped to shape each cohort's values and aspirations.

After gathering our data, we conducted hundreds of statistical tests to assess differences between our Gen X and Millennial samples. This book does not provide details about these analyses, which are available on request, but all the findings reported here met the standard for statistical significance. When we indicate, for example, that Millennial women are more likely to value helping others through their careers than their Gen X counterparts, this means that the chances of the pattern of responses observed in the two samples being the same is less than 5 percent, so we can conclude with confidence that the difference we observe is not occurring by random chance—that the Millennial women in our sample actually do care more about helping others than did the Gen Xers.

Many of our findings are not included in this book, but you can find simple descriptive statistics for responses to both surveys at www.worklife.wharton.upenn.edu. Finally, to fill out the picture, in 2012 we interviewed members of both the Class of 1992 and the Class of 2012. Select quotes from these interviews appear in the following pages.

In This Book

In chapter 1, I describe what we observed about the baby bust's context: the impact of the digital revolution, new pathways for early careers, definitions of success (for career and family) held by men and women, and the aspirations both have for their futures.

In the following two chapters, I explain why men and then women are now less likely to plan for children. For men, the key factors are an increase in anticipated conflict between work and other parts of life, a decrease in their identification with the role of breadwinner, and economic constraints due to debt. Women, on the other hand, are less likely to plan for children because of their increased focus on social impact, greater emphasis on building networks with friends and in their careers, changes in how they view their health, and a decrease in religious affiliation.

Chapter 4 compares, then and now, how men and women think about what "family" means and their relationships with their life partners. A crucial finding here is that men and women now share more common ground in their attitudes and aspirations about work and family than in the past.

In the final chapter, I provide ideas for actions we can all take—as a society, in our businesses, as individuals, and in our families—that I hope will inspire you to think and act differently. And there is a section specifically addressed to men. The conclusion is an invitation for you to join in this voyage of discovery.

I believe there is great opportunity for us to make things better, now and for future generations. Our progress as a society depends on our taking intelligent action now to increase the range of possibilities for men and women, at all stages of their lives, to pursue what matters most to them. It will not be easy, because much of what's needed involves cultural change. And that is accelerated by a clear-eyed awareness of how the world is different now.

CHAPTER 1

How We Got Here

*I wonder if it's worth having kids
when you aren't there to raise them.*

—Female, Class of 2012

The past 20 years have seen a radical transformation in the business landscape. Before digging into why young men and women are now less inclined to have children, which we'll do in the next two chapters, let's look at how much the ground has shifted. In this chapter, I'll describe what we observed about how the context in which these plans are being made has altered.

Life in the Digital Age

Technology has transformed nearly everything about all of our lives in the past 20 years, so it was naturally a major theme in the interviews we conducted in 2012 with members of both cohorts.

I wouldn't be surprised if you told me only half of us even had a PC [in 1992]. Cell phones didn't come on until three, four years later. And I still remember when I was that guy at the investment bank looking over the résumés deciding who got the interview. I remember the kids who would put their cell phone number on the résumé, I thought they were obnoxious, because why are they so important that I have to call their cell phone? Why can't I just call them at their dorm room? And now obviously no one has a dorm room phone number.

—Male, Class of 1992 (interviewed in 2012)

Life today is conducted at warp speed. Young people especially, having grown up in an accelerating world, expect instant access and gratification. Technology divides attention and makes it easy to move on if a task gets too boring. All this has caused many Millennials to expect to be constantly engaged and entertained. As one 2012 graduate told us, "I feel offended when things take a while." This sentiment was echoed by others.

This fierce urgency is good training for a business world where urgency itself is often paramount. As one Gen Xer in our study put it:

> *The speed of business is remarkably faster. Cycles are happening in months and years, not decades. The changes in technology from when I graduated to today are unbelievable.*

—*Male, Class of 1992 (interviewed in 2012)*

On the one hand, technology has crushed the boundaries of downtime, and on the other, it's helped to reduce barriers that once limited participation in business and social movements. The Internet and social media allow products and ideas to travel faster and farther, and anyone can now have a voice online. Access to information and knowledge is no longer reserved for the privileged few. For the students in our sample this means a reduction in status advantages and an increase in competition.

But the thirst for speed also has an inevitable effect on human relationships, and all the 1992 and 2012 graduates we interviewed spoke of these changes in their business and personal lives. Yes, technology has made the world simultaneously smaller and more open, but there is far less face-to-face interaction. This, in turn, has made communication a less personal, and perhaps even less truly social, activity. Here's how one 2012 graduate phrased what we heard from so many others:

> *It becomes a little bit more impersonal, because now you're texting instead of calling. Before, you had to call people's*

parents and say, "Hey, can Johnny come out and play in the neighborhood?" And she screams up to Johnny, and he comes running down the stairs, and they go play in the neighborhood. You're not interacting face-to-face. We're people; we're meant to interact with each other, not with a computer screen or with a keyboard.

—*Male, Class of 2012*

Early Careers—Indebted, Faster, Smarter, and More Absorbed

It's not only communications that are speeding up and becoming more intense; careers are, too. Saddled with greater debt, young people are now starting their adult work lives sooner and moving more rapidly between and among work settings. They are smarter about what it takes to succeed, and they are immersed in "extreme jobs" that require more of their time.

Handicapped by Debt

Compared to their 1992 counterparts, today's grads bear greater burdens from financing their educations, as others, too, have observed.[8] Millennials were more likely than Gen Xers to have financed their educations through employment and the use of scholarships and grants. While use of the most onerous type of student debt, private loans, has been cut in half over the past 20 years, the economic constraints that accompany debt still powerfully shape how Millennials envision their future careers and families, as we shall see.

Faster Out of the Gate

As the race to the top becomes more intense, young people around the world are increasingly trying to gain a head-start over their peers by getting early work experience. Between 1992 and 2012, Wharton students' participation in formal internship programs more than doubled—part of a national trend.[9] Gone are the days when young people could spend their summer breaks clerking in a local store or working a temporary white- or blue-collar job to earn some money. Today's students are narrowly targeting internship opportunities at top companies that fall within their fields of interest. They want to gain specific skills and connections that will help launch their careers.

Participation in formal internship programs grew so much over the past 20 years that it's now nearly universal. In the summer before their senior year of college, fully 78 percent of 2012 graduates, compared to 34 percent of those from 1992, held a formal internship. During the summer after their freshman year, twice as many 2012 respondents did, compared to two decades earlier. As one said:

> *The internships you have during college play a large role in determining what career paths you take. This is not necessarily because I have loved my work over the past few summers, but much more so because potential employers only consider you for positions similar to what you have had in the past.*

—*Male, Class of 2012*

The pressure to find career-related summer employment has also increased. In the summer following their junior year, only 34 percent of 1992 respondents were working in the industry they planned (at the time) to join; among 2012 respondents, this number was 53 percent. In a tight economy, internships today are increasingly seen as a near necessity.

Higher Mobility, Lower Stability

Young people expected greater competition in the labor market, and they anticipated that their career transitions would come in quicker succession. Between 1992 and 2012, expected first-job tenure fell from 3.4 to 2.0 years, and expected tenure at one's first organization fell from 4.6 to 3.7 years, similar to national labor market patterns.[10] Today's young people expect to be less attached to their employers.

Several trends may be contributing to today's high early-career mobility. With decreased hiring, many recent graduates are simply looking to get their foot in the door[11]—and they may be planning to move on to the job they really want a few years down the road, when they have built their résumés and skills. We saw some evidence for this. While only 25 percent of recent graduates believed their first job would, to a great extent, afford them the opportunity to express their passion, 52 percent of graduates predicted that their jobs 10 years in the future would do so. While these students may have settled for less desirable jobs at graduation, they expected to move on to more fulfilling work. One Millennial explained:

> *Our career paths seem to be structured around opportunities that emphasize working in a rigorous environment to gain exposure to an industry and to develop a skill set that is transferrable, with the ultimate hope that we can one day leverage this experience to move into a job that is more specific to our actual interests and desired lifestyle.*

—*Female, Class of 2012*

Apart from economics, another cause could be changes in attitudes, although there is some disagreement about how to characterize Millennials.[12] But most concur that Millennials are more likely to switch jobs. "Surfing" the labor market at a quick pace helps satisfy their need to be constantly stimulated and rewarded.[13]

Greater mobility may also be a by-product of "emerging adulthood" having become a more commonplace and socially accepted stage in life, one that involves delaying the roles and responsibilities traditionally associated with adulthood and settling down—that is, getting married, buying a home, and starting a family. One 2012 graduate explained the pressure she felt to explore different job options:

> *There is an expectation among my generation that our career paths will be changing and convoluted. Especially in the first ten years out of college, we are nearly expected to "job-hop" every few years, gaining broad-based experiences as we hope to identify the passion we would like to pursue in our thirties. While such an expectation is liberating in the sense that it frees us from the urgency and responsibility to choose and commit to a career path early on, I feel that such expectations challenge an overall sense of purpose and purposefulness in our career decisions.*

> *—Female, Class of 2012*

Another new norm is the shifting focus from long-term employment toward "employability." As downsizing and displacement have become more pressing concerns for everyone, young people are unwilling to think of their careers as existing solely within a single organization. Frequent moves allow people to build a more diverse set of skills and connections, making it easier to find a new job if their position gets terminated.[14]

Bottom line: The students we surveyed in 2012 were not expecting permanence.

Smarter about the Game

Today's young people are savvier about the social aspects of what it takes to get ahead in the business world. Certainly the exposure gained through internships has opened their eyes to such matters. Hailing generally from families that were better educated and

wealthier than those of their Gen X counterparts, and more likely to
have had both parents employed, our Millennials also had the benefit
of greater parental experience with what leads to career success.

Graduates in 2012 were less likely than their 1992 counterparts
to believe that their undergraduate grades would play a pivotal role
in their careers. Instead, they were more able to envision their careers
as being built on relationships as the currency for success. The Class
of 2012 was more likely than the Class of 1992 to agree that they
would need to make their superiors aware of their accomplishments
in order to further their careers. And they were also more aware of
how they would need to build a web of relationships to further their
advancement.[15]

More Absorbed in Extreme Jobs

Greater competition means more than just elbowing for room at the
starting line and moving faster across organizational boundaries.
Compared to their peers of 20 years ago, respondents in 2012
expected that they would need to devote far more time to work—
about 14 more hours each week. While 1992 graduates going into
full-time work expected, on average, a 58-hour workweek, those in
2012 planned to work 72 hours per week.

This expectation of longer work hours coincides with observed
changes in workplace norms, particularly among those in highly
paid jobs. Hewlett and Luce, in a study of "extreme jobs," found that
for high-earning individuals (the top 6 percent of U.S. earners),
the 72-hour workweek that 2012 grads are expecting is not unusual.
A 60-hour week, once a sure path to the top, is now considered
practically part time. Among workers in jobs that require 24/7
availability, careers have become ever more intensely absorbing.[16]

For the most ambitious business graduates, wherever they
attend school, there are more competitors and fewer trophies. People
understand that they need to do more to set themselves apart.

The Road More Traveled

As the undergraduates in our surveys have quickened the pace of their careers, collectively they have also narrowed their focus. They now pursue a more limited number of industries and are more likely to follow a structured, predefined career path. The top two most popular industries in 1992, investment banking/financial services and consulting, drew in just under half (45 percent) of all Wharton graduates. Twenty years later nearly three-quarters (72 percent) of 2012 graduates selected jobs in one of these two industries. And our peer institutions are finding the same to be true of their recent undergraduates.[17]

Other industries that drew a significant number of new graduates in 1992 (accounting, law, and medicine/health care) were hardly mentioned by the Class of 2012. When asked about changes they would like to see to the architecture of careers, several 2012 grads commented on the pressure to enter a limited number of fields:

> *I would structure it so that students don't have to go straight into investment banking or consulting in order to have exit opportunities. There would be less of a herd mentality.*

> —Male, Class of 2012

Several 2012 respondents noted that accepted standards of career timing,[18] combined with a funneling of industry options, left them feeling as though they had little choice when it came to their career paths. As one of them put it, again speaking for others as well:

> *There is not much creativity or desire to stray from this path, and everyone believes that two years in banking or consulting is a necessary evil before they either return to graduate school or find their dream job.*

> —Male, Class of 2012

Add it all together—the debt load before a career is even launched, the pressure and uncertainty of early careers, and the diminished potential for face-to-face interaction—and a diminished focus on families and children might seem almost inevitable, but that's still only part of the story.

Narrowing of the Gender Gap

Today's graduating seniors feel greater constraints on their career paths and feel less able to shape their futures in a way that both fits their espoused values and allows them to foresee rich work and family lives. But we have also seen some distinct positive changes over the past 20 years. Most notably, women have achieved professional parity with men, at least at the start of their careers.

The most obvious leveling is in starting salaries. While men in 1992 earned over $5,000 more per year in their first jobs than their female peers, in 2012 there was no difference between men and women in first-job salary. Perhaps even more telling than salary numbers was this observation: women now perceive themselves to be on an even footing with their male peers. In 1992, men rated their first-job salaries as higher than the class average, and women rated theirs as lower than those of their peers. By 2012, however, this gender gap in perceptions had disappeared. Men and women were no different in how they believed their first-job salary measured up to those of their classmates. Today's young women do not see themselves as being at a disadvantage.

Other aspects of men's and women's career plans have also converged. While in 1992 men expected to work four more hours each week than did their female peers, there is no longer a gender gap in expected time at work. Men and women now agree also on career timing—whereas Gen X women expected to spend less time at their first jobs and first organizations than did their male peers, both sexes now hold similar views about the timing of their first few career moves. And while men and women had significantly different educational goals in 1992, they now have comparable plans when it comes to obtaining postgraduate education.

In sum, as they start out, today's Wharton men and women have the same expectations about initial salaries, how much of their time will be spent working, career mobility, and their further education.

Success and Happiness

Changes in technology and the work world have created dramatic new life challenges and opportunities for college graduates. Values are the compass that graduates use to navigate this rapidly evolving terrain, and here, too, we saw fascinating shifts in how young people define what it means to be successful. We examined values by asking participants in our study to indicate both the importance (on a scale of 1 to 5) of 12 life success factors (e.g., health, religion, wealth) and of 15 career success factors (e.g., money, enjoyment, challenge), and their satisfaction, or happiness, with each one. I'll describe here some of the changes in both the rank order and the absolute value of the ratings made by our respondents on these success factors. For details, visit www.worklife.wharton.upenn.edu.

Women Are Happier Than Men

Gen X men and women were equally satisfied with all aspects of their lives at the time of their graduation. But for Millennials, women were happier than their male classmates in terms of health, personal growth, and friends. Over the past 20 years, a gap has formed between men's and women's happiness with these critical aspects of their lives.

Long-Term Relationships, Children, and Friends

We saw in the life success rankings a decrease in the relative importance Millennials placed on both long-term relationships and parenting compared to their Gen X counterparts. Nonetheless, parenting is still highly valued by young people today, even if relatively less so. Similarly, while the relative importance of having time for family dropped in how people assess their career success, it was still a critical consideration.

Compared to the Class of 1992, Millennials considered friendships a more important factor in determining the success of their lives; friends now rank second only to one's health. Women in both cohorts considered friendships significantly more important than did their male peers. In a related finding, Millennials were more likely than Gen Xers to feel that their undergraduate years had helped them develop the ability to make friends. In chapter 4 we'll look more closely at what these observations tell us about emergent conceptions of family.

Social Impact

The past 20 years have seen a surge of interest among women in making a positive difference in the world, and not just in our sample.[19] Between 1992 and 2012, Wharton women became more likely to agree that helping others is an important aspect of career success. And in judging the success of their lives and careers, they now rate helping others higher than do men. There was no difference between men and women in 1992.

Respect and Status

While others also find that Millennials as a whole are more motivated by social recognition in their careers than Gen Xers,[20] we found that this trend has been driven mainly by changes in women. Young women in 2012 valued careers that afforded social status and prestige as well as respect by others more so than did their 1992 counterparts. While men and women both valued social recognition equally in 1992, women are now significantly more focused on these aspects of a career than are men.[21] Over the past 20 years, women seem to have recognized that they need not just initial access to business society but also status and respect; the glass ceiling has come into sharper focus.

Time for Self

Millennials in general, but especially women, were more likely than their Gen X counterparts to value careers that allowed them to have time to themselves—and no wonder, given the drastic increase in expected time at work.

Power and Hierarchical Advancement

Millennials were more likely than Gen Xers to believe that career success means having power and influence and advancing rapidly to a high-level position. But, as we'll see, desire for hierarchical advancement doesn't necessarily translate into actual expectations for achieving it.

Standard of Living and Job Security

Millennials in our study placed a higher value on standard of living (what money can buy) than did those who graduated in 1992. Conditioned by new technology that includes both public knowledge of consumer activity and instant gratification, perhaps Millennials are quicker to fulfill their material desires for social display.

The Class of 2012 also cared more about job security than did their counterparts from 20 years ago. But students' *current economic position* had no relation to the importance they placed on job security. Class of 2012 members who had accumulated student debt through government or private loans were no more likely than those who did not have such debt to value job security. And those who were dissatisfied with their current level of material wealth and standard of living similarly did not care about job security any more than did their well-off peers. Compared to 1992, students on all socioeconomic levels were more focused on job security in 2012.

Career Aspirations

We've seen how much has changed in the way young people are thinking about their plans for children. And we've explored what's been altered as a result of the digital revolution, the economic pressures now felt by new entrants to the business professional labor market, and the things they value in their lives. But what about their actual plans for their careers?

The Economics of Future Career Plans—Student Debt and Job Security

Economic concerns played a large role in shaping how Millennials saw their professional futures. Student debt constrained young men's short-term aspirations. Men in the Class of 2012 who had had to work their way through college believed they were less likely to achieve a sense of meaning in their early careers by having a positive impact. Those who had worked to pay their tuition were less likely to predict that their first job would allow them to make a contribution to the world and serve others.

A recurring complaint was that the necessity of paying back student loans was forcing them into career paths they wouldn't otherwise choose:

> *Career decisions are based on how much money a student owes due to tuition. I'd much rather have been a physicist, but that would mean paying student loans for 30 years.*

> *—Male, Class of 2012*

But a different kind of economic concern (job security) constrained young men's forecasts about finding meaning in their careers later in the game. While Millennial men's expectations for their jobs 10 years after graduation were unaffected by student debt and student employment, their concern for job security affected whether they believed they might attain meaningful jobs 10 years after graduation—jobs with a sense of purpose and with the opportunity to express a passion.

Young men with an initial monetary disadvantage have modified their career plans accordingly, shifting the focus away from finding meaningful work and toward making money. But they expected that their disadvantage wouldn't last forever and that they would be able to engage in work that matters in the future. On the other hand, those who valued job security expected long-term trade-offs; they were less likely to believe that their work would provide a sense of meaning far down the road. Student debt can eventually be overcome, but the mind-set forged by coming of age during a recession might well have a lasting impact on Millennials.

Lowered Ambitions

When predicting how their professional lives will actually unfold, Millennials were less optimistic about their future attainments than their Gen X peers. Compared to their predecessors from the Class of 1992, recent graduates expected to be less elite in virtually all aspects of their careers—including their future salaries, hierarchical advancement, and educational achievements.

Members of the Class of 2012, for example, were less likely than Gen Xers to say that their salary in their first job was above the class average. And this generational drop in expectations extends into more distant career planning. More than half (52 percent) of Gen Xers said they would be earning more money than their classmates 10 years after graduating; this compares to just 39 percent of Millennials.

The most recent cohort of students was also significantly more pessimistic about its ability to climb the corporate ladder. In 1992, 55 percent of graduates said they would try to become the top-level executive within a firm, compared to 39 percent in

2012. Some researchers are finding that young people are now less inclined to reach for greater responsibility at work and instead are preferring saner hours and more time for nonwork.[22] But we are finding, additionally, that even though they held lower hierarchical aspirations, Millennials rated themselves as less likely to achieve even their considerably lowered goals.

Millennials were also less ambitious than Gen Xers when it came to educational pursuits. While 85 percent of 1992 graduates planned to attain a graduate-level degree, only 76 percent of 2012 graduates planned the same.

Several factors may explain Millennials' diminished career aspirations. Greater awareness of today's intensely competitive business environment could be leading them to lower their career goals to more attainable levels. The turn away from entrepreneurship—which offers high risk and potentially high reward—that we observed in this undergraduate sample over the past 20 years may also be responsible for lower hierarchical aspirations. It might be that because so many 2012 grads plan to stick to established corporations, they cannot reasonably expect to reach the same levels as their more entrepreneurial predecessors. Another possibility is that the rising focus on job security over the past 20 years means that Millennials are less likely to make high-risk, high-payoff career moves.

"Only a Life Lived for Others Is a Life Worthwhile"

Albert Einstein said that, and he'd probably be pleased to know that there is one aspect of their careers that Millennials value that does indeed seem attainable: Those who want to establish careers that benefit society and those who defined life success as helping others believe they will be able to do so in their future jobs, 10 years after graduation.

While today's young people may feel unable to achieve all their professional and family goals, they feel confident in their ability to make a positive social impact. Even so, Millennials are strikingly aware of limitations and external constraints. To a greater degree than Gen Xers, Millennials who wanted to help others through their careers expected to earn less money in their first jobs and in their jobs 10 years after graduation. Millennials may be more idealistic about healing the broken world, but they are quite realistic about the earnings penalties for trying to do so.

At the same time, for those in the Class of 1992 and the men (but not women) in 2012 who defined career success as helping others, earning a great deal of money was less important to their life and career success. For these groups, the financial hit associated with helping others seems to be an acceptable trade-off. However, for Millennial women who want careers that have a positive social impact, wealth and salary continue to be highly valued. Unlike their male counterparts, these women seem to be struggling to sort through competing priorities—in this case, helping others versus wealth accumulation; and in another case, as we'll see in chapter 3, helping others versus becoming mothers.

The baby bust we've observed has not occurred in a vacuum. Decisions about whether to have children depend on a constellation of social, cultural, and economic forces that shape almost infinite calculations, conscious and unconscious. Now that we've reviewed some of those forces, we can turn to the specific reasons the Millennial men in our study were dramatically less likely than their Gen X counterparts to become fathers.

Summing Up

- The technological revolution has changed the nature of our relationships and increased the speed and competitiveness of today's business world.
- Burdened with greater debt than those in earlier generations, young college graduates today have often started their careers

early via interning, are preparing to move rapidly between jobs, and are steeling themselves for "extreme jobs"—expecting to work an average of 14 more hours per week.

- While young people still value family life, in defining success, the Class of 2012 ranked having time for family, long-term relationships, and parenting relatively lower than did the Class of 1992.
- The Millennials in our study were less optimistic about their future career attainments than their Gen X peers and cared more about job security. Nevertheless, those looking to make a positive social impact were sanguine about their prospects for doing so.

CHAPTER 2

Why Fewer Men Plan to Have Children Now

At the end of the day it's your family that you want to spend time with and you want to see them happy, but at the same time you want to provide for them. So I want to work hard to be a provider.

—Male, Class of 1992 (interviewed in 2012)

In this chapter, we concentrate on the reasons the Millennial men in our study are dramatically less likely than their Gen X counterparts to become fathers: the anticipated conflict between work and the rest of life; changes in gender role stereotypes, especially about men's role as breadwinner; and economic concerns.

How Can I Be an Involved Dad and Have a Great Career?

Not surprisingly, men in both our 1992 and 2012 surveys who expected to have trouble managing the competing demands of work and family were less inclined to have children than those with high expectations of being able to "have it all."

In 1992, intentions to become a father were lowest among those men who said that:

- Pursuing a demanding career would make it more difficult for them to be an attentive spouse/partner
- Being a parent would limit their career success
- Competing demands of work and life would force them to decide which is more important

While expected work-family conflict still deters young men from planning to have children, just as it did 20 years ago, the intensity of such anticipated conflicts for men (and women, too, for that matter) has increased. Men in 1992 believed that they could have demanding careers and still have families, while men in 2012 were more inclined to doubt that proposition.[23]

Part of this increase in expected conflict has been driven by the anticipation of large increases in work hours. Millennial men who foresaw extreme job requirements were likely to believe that a demanding career would make it difficult for them to be attentive spouses and partners. In addition, anticipating these overwhelming hours, they were less confident in their ability to make career decisions that would allow them to stay true to themselves and their values.

But it's not only the anticipation of longer, more demanding workdays that is contributing to the baby bust among men. Men of this hard-charging generation, even more so than in previous cohorts, are racing onto career tracks that are notoriously arduous. As these young men expect to work longer hours, and as technology makes it increasingly difficult to delineate the boundary between work and home, it is little wonder they would expect greater conflict between work and family than their 1992 counterparts. Men today expect to play more active roles at home than Gen X men did and they are more likely to expect their spouses to be employed. It's hard to do everything if you're really going to put your heart and soul into it, and today's young men seem to understand that.

In short, they appear to be moving into the future with their eyes wide open. A 2012 study participant who told us that, as he looked well into his future, he foresaw "struggling [with] how to advance in my career while balancing the extremely important component in life of raising and spending time with my family" is typical of many of his classmates. Rather than simply considering whether they want to have children, young men today are increasingly asking themselves whether they will be able to raise children successfully while pursuing their career goals—and increasingly answering this question with a "no" by opting out of fatherhood. And, compared to men in 1992, those in 2012 reported that long-term relationships were less important to them.

So it was not surprising to find a generational change in the percentages of men in the four categories of "life role priority": career-oriented (career is primary), family-oriented (family is primary), career- and family-oriented (both are equally valued), or self- and society-oriented (neither family nor career is primary). We found that men in 2012 were more oriented toward career and self and society and less toward family than those in 1992. The percentage of career-oriented men had more than doubled, while the percentage in the family-oriented category had fallen by more than one-quarter. There was also a decline in the percentage of career- and family-oriented types. While more than half (54 percent) of Gen X men belonged in this category, placing equal priority on work and family, only 45 percent of Millennial men did.

Not Your Father's Father

In addition to our finding that young men are less inclined to plan to become fathers, shifts in gender roles over the past two decades have reframed the meaning of fatherhood for young men in three important ways. First, the prevalence of working mothers gives these men a different perspective on having and rearing children. Second, prospective fathers are less inclined to construe their roles in the ways their fathers did. Third, today's young men now associate having a positive social impact with playing a more active role at home; they understand the import of their involvement in raising the next generation—it's serious and it's daunting.

Having a Working Mother No Longer Affects Whether Men Plan to Have Children

Our 1992 survey found that a mother's participation in the workforce affected her son's (but not her daughter's) plans to become a parent. Back then, men who were raised in what might have been termed traditional households—with a mother at home full time in the early years of their lives—were more likely to plan to have children of their own than those whose mothers worked outside the home. But that difference disappeared between 1992 and 2012, during which time there was more than a twofold increase in the percentage of those in our study who were raised by employed mothers.

For Millennial men, unlike their counterparts two decades earlier, whether their mother worked had no bearing on their plans to opt into fatherhood, likely because this family arrangement has become normative.[24]

Men No Longer See Themselves as the Sole Breadwinner

Historically, men were able to find a common thread and little conflict between work and family because both involved taking on the role of breadwinner. Those men who were seeking the most out of their careers were the most likely to plan to become fathers because they saw their jobs as a means of supporting their families. Their drive to succeed professionally was motivated by a desire to provide for future children; therefore, observable external indicators of career progress were markers of their success in both the work and the family spheres. Twenty years later, that psychological link is attenuated in the minds of young men. Their careers and the money they earn in their jobs are not tightly tied to providing for children. In many ways, men in 1992 were still dyed-in-the-wool traditionalists when it came to having children and in their role as breadwinner. We found, for example, that expectations of fatherhood back then were most common among those who valued careers that afforded:

- Achieving social status and prestige
- Earning a great deal of money
- Advancing rapidly to high-level positions
- Living in a preferred geographical area
- Attaining a high standard of living
- Obtaining material wealth

Additional evidence on how external markers of career success were part of the father-to-be mind-set: those men in 1992 who believed their first-job salaries were higher than their classmates' were also more likely to plan to have children. This suggests that, two decades ago, men who valued material success and were confident in their abilities to provide wealth were more likely to plan to have children. Gen X men saw themselves as breadwinners and pursued careers with the intention of providing for a family; this was all one seamless, conflict-free mind-set. But for business-minded, upwardly mobile men today, the connection between all these indicators of success and the intention to become a father has vanished.

Another finding helps us understand how changes in men's and women's roles have affected the plans of young men to become fathers. In 2012, young men who believed that two-career relationships work best when "neither partner has stereotypical or traditional ideas about men's and women's family roles" were significantly more likely to be planning to have children than those who didn't share this view. Not so in 1992. Furthermore, those Millennial men who held this view were more likely to value flexibility in work hours; another indication of their interest in fatherhood.

Today, it is those men who are willing to step outside the breadwinner role—those inclined to challenge traditional assumptions and, for instance, actively share in family life—who are choosing to have children. Now men with traditional views are the ones who are less likely to become fathers. Given the reality that today's women are planning to work, these "traditionalist" men find it harder to see how a family life that includes children is going to work out for them.

But, to be sure, old stereotypes linger. One man said:

> *I do feel like there is an expectation in that it's more normal for the male to work. A part of me will always be challenging and fighting that. But more and more people—the males in the relationship, the husbands—are staying home to be the primary caregiver. So that's changing. This is a conversation that comes up a lot.*

—Male, Class of 2012

Making a Positive Social Impact via Fatherhood

"My dream job," said one student at the start of one of my fall 2012 classes, "is to be a stay-at-home dad." And our surveys along with other studies show that his wasn't a lone voice in the wilderness.

The conversation has changed. Men no longer expect to fill the breadwinner role, and most see traditional gender roles (that is, women taking care of the children) in dual-career relationships as antagonistic to their becoming fathers because they know that women will be working. Other researchers have shown that while fathers continue to spend less time on child care than mothers, they are spending more time with their children than their own fathers did.[25] The young men in our study who expect to have children do not see the primary responsibility of fatherhood as bringing home the bacon. These young men expect and want to be involved dads.

As we'll see in the next chapter, young women over the last two decades have uncoupled the desire to do good in the world from the desire for motherhood. Not so for men and fatherhood. Young men of both cohorts who wanted to have a positive social impact anticipated doing so, at least in part, by rearing the next generation. But in 2012 we saw evidence of a strong link between prospective fathers being engaged with their families and their making a positive difference in society.

We found, for example, that men in 2012 who valued helping others were less likely to foresee (a) the demands of family life interfering with their achieving success in their careers, (b) pursuing a demanding career making it difficult for them to be an attentive spouse or partner, and (c) having to make sacrifices in the personal and family lives to achieve success in their careers. In other words, for those young men who place a high value on making a positive difference in the world, work and family are compatible; they are neither antagonistic nor problematic.

Similarly, those young men who cared about helping others through their work and lives were more likely to agree that they would be able to "have it all." The more socially conscious men felt confident that they would be able to have rich business lives and be successful as husbands and fathers. One such grad from the Class of 2012, who was going to work for a program that places enterprising college grads in start-ups focused on revitalizing communities, said this:

> *If my future wife is doing something that she loves, then I want her to keep doing that and we'll make it work with the kids. I'm no expert in parenting, but I would assume that it's a lot of compromise. It's a lot of understanding that we're going to miss some of the bigger moments in a kid's life. Instead of hearing my kid say his first word, maybe it's her, or maybe it's the person at the day care center.*

—*Male, Class of 2012*

While the lives of young men today are intensely entwined in their careers and the pursuit of material comfort, it's not all about the money, even for those young men who have been training to enter business from an early age. But make no mistake—money still plays a key role in determining whether men embrace fatherhood or shy away from it.

I Owe, I Owe, It's Off to Work I Go

When we asked students in 2012 to predict their lives 20 years in the future, economic uncertainties were rarely far from their plans or their thoughts. As one Millennial told us:

> *I hope to have a successful career that will allow me to achieve financial security for myself and my family. I want to be able to provide my children with all the resources necessary for them to achieve their full potential and be happy.*

—*Male, Class of 2012*

Weakened though it may be, the enduring link between young men and the breadwinner role means that they are particularly susceptible to economic difficulties, perhaps most notably student debt. It is the millstone that so many college graduates wear around their necks as they venture into the working world. It is a burden that has a powerful effect on parenting decisions. Chris Christopher, senior economist at IHS Global Insight, calls student debt "a real monkey wrench in the works of our families and economy," adding that if college costs and student debt continue to rise, the nation's low birthrate may become the "new normal."[26]

Nobel Prize–winning economist Joseph E. Stiglitz concurs. Nationwide, the average debt of seniors graduating with outstanding loans exceeds $26,000, he writes, but "an 'average' like this masks huge variations." One in seven student loan borrowers owes more than $50,000, and one in 25 more than $100,000, and these are figures unlikely to improve in the short or long term. "Those with huge debts are likely to be cautious before undertaking the additional burdens of a family," Stiglitz adds.[27]

The students we surveyed tend to become relatively high earners, and one might expect, therefore, that they would be buffered from the harshness of this national trend. But on this score, what's true in general is also true of the Wharton Class of 2012. The men who said they had financed their undergraduate educations through employment, private loans, government loans, and scholarships and grants were significantly less likely to plan to have children. Money matters: Today's young men understand that raising children, and surely sending them to school, is expensive. They are therefore less willing to take on this responsibility, and are holding back accordingly. Because they carry debt forward from their school to their working years, even for those near the top of the ladder compared to their peers nationally, it's not surprising that young men who face years of indebtedness may be uncertain about taking on the cost of children.

While 2012 men no longer identify their values with the breadwinner role, many men still identify with and worry about their ability to fulfill this role's financial obligations. These seemingly contradictory observations—that men no longer think of themselves as breadwinners but are still anxious about their ability to support their kids—indicates that we are in a period of transition as men's and women's roles converge. Men aren't sure who they are or how to be.

Take note that this concern about the financial risks inhibiting plans for fatherhood, like the others discussed in this chapter, is specific to men: Wharton women in 2012 who financed their educations through government loans were more likely to plan to become mothers. It's another story for women today, both compared to men and to the world women were entering two decades ago. Money matters to them, too, of course, but in a different way, as we'll see in the next chapter.

Summing Up

- As in the past, men who expect their work and family lives to clash are more likely to opt out of fatherhood. But men today are anticipating more conflict between the different aspects of their lives, so they are abstaining from parenting in larger numbers than those a generation earlier did.

- Having a working mother no longer affects whether a man plans to become a father himself, as it did a generation ago.
- Men are also less inclined than their own fathers to think of themselves as breadwinners, with all the commitments that entails. Their conceptions of their roles are changing.
- Doing good and rearing a family are linked in the minds of today's young men. Those who want to help others expect greater harmony between their work and family lives.
- Faced with increasing amounts of debt, young men today are more averse than earlier generations to invest in children.

CHAPTER 3

Why Fewer Women Plan to Have Children Now

I hope I have a family, with or without children,
that is stable and is a source of happiness in my life,
but I would be surprised if I stopped my career entirely
to have children at any point.

—*Female, Class of 2012*

Back in 1992, women in the very top echelons of organizations were rarer than black swans, but change was on the horizon. The looming high-tech boom would soon provide new routes for rapid female advancement—and, for some, unimaginable wealth.

That spirit of awakening is evident in our findings from two decades ago. For the most part, these Gen X women placed high value on enjoyable work and challenging tasks, and they had no *intention* of opting out of the workforce. They had worked hard for their degrees and knew the value of the education they had received.

Today's young women have retained a focus on their careers, but have different attitudes about what's important in their lives. They are more likely than those who came before them to define career success in terms of being respected, having time for themselves, advancing rapidly to high-level positions, enjoying great prestige, helping others, or (the biggest jumps of all) having power and influence and a secure job. At the same time, as we've seen, Millennial women are much less inclined toward motherhood. Nine in 10 women in the Class of 1992 told us that they planned to have or adopt children

(79 percent) or probably would (12 percent). By 2012, only slightly more than half the women in the Wharton Class of 2012 were planning to do so—41 percent said they would and 14 percent said they probably would.

Another big difference: For both men and women in 1992 but for men only in 2012, the importance placed on parenting was linked to one's plans for having children. If one valued parenthood, then one was very likely to be planning to become a parent. However, for women in 2012, those who valued parenting as an important part of life—and they were numerous—were no more likely to plan to have children than those who didn't think that being a parent was so important. Today, for young women the desire to be a mother doesn't lead to a plan to become one.

Why this radical shift? The constellation of converging forces affecting ambitious young women is quite different from that affecting men's plans, as I'll address in this chapter. We found two seemingly contradictory things occurring at once. On the one hand—and this is progress—Millennial women are no longer bound by outmoded expectations that they be the primary nurturers at home and are freer to make choices based on their own unique strengths, talents, and desires as they contemplate work and family matters. At the same time, however, we observed that they are also acutely aware of the external pressures (time, money, and more) that constrain their options, so that those who value parenting cannot readily figure out how to make motherhood a reality. For women today, as with men, it's complicated.

Whom to Serve—My Own Children or the Family of Humankind?

While 2012 grads as a group were more concerned about social issues than those in 1992, young women in particular have developed a stronger interest in solving social problems, and many see no impediment to doing so within the context of a high-powered business career. As one woman said:

> I would hope in twenty years I would be having a positive impact on the world...I truly believe that industry can be positive for the world. That's not necessarily a viewpoint that is shared by many people, especially the public. But corporate social responsibility, operations management, having efficient systems and processes— these things matter. Doing good business does not have to be mutually exclusive with doing good in the environment. In fact, I think that they can go hand in hand.

—*Female, Class of 2012*

Idealism and youth have always gone hand in hand, but Millennial women in our study have stepped it up to a new level—apparently at the expense of motherhood. Not only were these recent female grads more likely than their 1992 counterparts and their Class of 2012 male peers to define career success as helping others, but we also found that young women who expected their jobs 10 years in the future to provide the chance to serve others were significantly less likely to plan to become mothers.

For these young, business-minded women, there seems to be a trade-off between rearing the next generation in one's own family and serving the family of humankind, and herein lies a critical difference between the Gen X and the Millennial women we surveyed. Social consciousness now competes with motherhood: making a contribution to the world has become an increasingly common means for women to achieve a sense of meaning and purpose. In 1992, women who defined success in work and life as helping others were also likely to place high value on being a parent; back then, helping others meant being a mother.

By 2012, however, no such connections between women's altruism and their valuation of parenting remained. Just as gender roles for men are changing, with young men no longer hewing so closely to the breadwinner model, so, too, young women are less constrained by the societal expectation that to be a good, caring, and nurturing woman means one has to bear and care for one's own children.

This conclusion is reinforced by other results on women's changing attitudes about their careers. In 1992, women who valued helping others through their work were also likely to care about those aspects of a job that were conducive to motherhood: flexibility in work hours, time for family, and a secure job. By contrast, women in 2012 who wanted to help others in their careers were likely to value those aspects of a job that would give them a sense of meaning and purpose in their work: challenging tasks, opportunities for expressing creativity, and power and influence.

The paradigm shift is evident. For Gen X women, to help others was to be a mother, while for 2012 women, to help others is to succeed in producing social impact through their careers. Women in both cohorts are nurturers, but the nature of their nurturing is taking different forms.

This change reflects the discourse currently taking place in American society. While intentionally childless adults have, in the recent past, been seen in a somewhat negative light, perhaps as "selfish," this attitude appears to have undergone a significant change over the last quarter century. In 1988, only 39 percent of Americans disagreed with the statement that childless adults "lead empty lives"; that is, the majority agreed with the statement. As of 2010 that number had swelled to 59 percent; in other words, now the majority disagree that childless adults lead "empty lives."[28] This shift is mirrored by a new vocabulary; many of the young women discussing their life choices today refer to themselves not as "childless" but as "childfree."[29]

Indeed among some women, the tide in perception seems to be shifting in the opposite direction—that parenthood, not childlessness, is the selfish choice. Today, in pondering whether to bring a child into the world, young people are considering the environmental impact, the effects on the child of struggling to live in an overpopulated world, and the knowledge that many children are not well cared for because not all adults are cut out to be nurturing parents.[30]

Instead of channeling their generative ambitions into motherhood, women are increasingly focusing on social involvement through the achievement of goals other than the pursuit of children.

But If I Am Having Children, One of Us Should Be Home

Perhaps not surprisingly, women who feel a strong calling toward making a broad social impact are also concerned with the well-being of their own children, if they are planning to have them. Indeed, in 2012 (but not in 1992), those women who placed high value on helping others were likely to believe that two-career relationships work best when one partner:

- is more advanced in his or her career
- stays home or works part time when their children are young

Furthermore, those Millennial women who want to help others expressed more negative attitudes about the impact of working parents on their children. They were more likely to believe that children whose:

- mothers are employed suffer because their mothers are not there when they need them
- fathers are employed suffer because their fathers are not there when they need them

Women who care about making the world a better place reported that children need their mothers and their fathers to be with them. What we found is that those women in 2012 who were focused on helping society saw motherhood as a constraint. They recognized the need for children to spend time with their parents and worried that this would limit their ability to make a difference in the world through their work. The anticipation of this constraint might explain why women intending to make a positive social impact were less willing to have children in the future; this is in contrast to men today, who see positive social impact and fatherhood going hand in hand.

My Friends Mean a Lot to Me

Not only are today's young women more focused on professional networks and their friends, but this increased interest in nonfamily social ties coincides with their lower likelihood of having children. For Millennial women (and men), being in networks and having access to alumni were more important considerations at college than for Gen Xers. And for the women in 2012, the more important that networking opportunities and access to alumni were, the less likely the women were to plan to have children. In a similar vein, those women who were especially glad that their college experience had helped them develop the ability to make friends were less likely to plan to have children.

The takeaway: Women are increasingly finding social satisfaction outside their families. Creating a biological family is becoming less of a necessity for their fulfillment and happiness. Social networks enable young professionals to feel a sense of connection. Networks support their career growth, too, through access to resources—a win-win proposition in the new calculus of many young female professionals.

I Don't Have to Have Children

We saw evidence that shows how women are now freer to choose to take care of themselves rather than feeling compelled to bear and care for children, as expected by traditional norms. As one 2012 grad put it:

I do not plan on having a family. I simply want to focus on becoming a top executive at a Fortune 100 company within the next twenty years.

—*Female, Class of 2012*

In one of the more surprising findings from our longitudinal study, we saw a reversal of the meaning of health as it relates to motherhood. The women in the Class of 1992 viewed their good health and prospective motherhood as mutually reinforcing; the more important health was to them, the more likely they were to plan to have children. However, those members of the Class of 2012 who placed high value on their health were *less* likely to plan to become mothers, perhaps because young women now equate physical health with fitness—which has gained exponentially in importance in our culture.[31] Recall also our earlier observation that Millennial women rated having time for themselves as more important than did Gen Xers. Knowing that having children will likely reduce the time available for taking care of themselves, more women are deciding it is not worth it.

Our observations about trends in religious affiliation also provide evidence of greater freedom of choice. The religious makeup of the Class of 2012 differed significantly from that of the Class of 1992, with the largest group now being agnostic (34 percent identified themselves thus in 2012, compared to only 12 percent in 1992); national trends are similar.[32] For women, the link between religious affiliation and one's plans for having children changed, too.[33] In 2012, women who identified as agnostic were significantly less likely to plan for children than other religious groups. In addition, women in 2012—but not those in 1992—who said that religion was important to them were more accepting of traditional roles at home; they were more likely to agree that, in a two-career relationship, one partner should be more advanced in his or her career than the other and one partner should stay home or work part time while the children were young. The increased number of women reporting that they are agnostic, and the fewer expectations for traditional women's roles associated with this belief system, were linked to more women deciding not to plan to have children.

In sum, our findings about how plans for children are related to women's views of health and traditional role expectations affirm the inference that the baby bust is, in part, an indication of greater freedom to choose. But for young women, as for young men, economic considerations are never far from the surface.

I Can't Afford Kids until My Career Is Set

While both men and women anticipate more conflict between work and other parts of life today, the increase over the past two decades has been greater for women. But, unlike for men, our study shows that anticipated conflict between work and family does not directly affect women's plans to have children. It seems that for these savvy young women, it's understood that there will be conflict between work and family; to them, the conflict is a given, like air and water, and thus does not explain or predict anything.

Still, the anticipation of such conflict is increasingly part of the mix of thoughts in which such decisions are made by women. The women we studied in 2012 were more likely than their 1992 counterparts to agree that:

- the demands of family life would interfere with achieving a successful career
- pursuing a demanding career would make it difficult to be an attentive spouse or partner
- competing demands of career and family would require that they decide which is more important
- being a parent would limit their career success

For women intent on a high-powered career, the biological realities—particularly the timing of when to have children—pose challenges specific to them. Is it best to have children early in one's career while one is most fertile but when one needs to establish career inroads; midstream, which might be one's last best chance to bear children but may irrevocably disrupt one's career trajectory; or perhaps not at all? Highly competitive and volatile job markets—the nature of the employment situation in recent years—only complicate the matter further, as does carrying debt forward from the college years.

A 2012 Pew Research Center study found that more than 1 in 5 young adults between the ages of 18 and 34 had delayed having a child because of the lagging economy. Similarly, a 2012 Rutgers University study found that 4 in 10 recent college graduates had delayed a major life decision, such as buying a house or having a child, due to debt.[34] Not surprisingly, these same concerns surfaced in our research.

We found that women (and men, too) in 2012 valued job security more highly than did people in 1992, a reflection of the current economic anxieties. And perhaps because of financial considerations, they are delaying parenthood: the ages at which young people plan to have children have increased significantly for women (and men) over the past 20 years. For women at least, this delay in childrearing is directly related to concerns about job security. In 1992, women who highly valued job security expected to have their youngest children at an earlier age than did those women for whom job security was not a great concern. In 2012, at least for one's second-youngest child, the opposite was true: women who emphasized job security, compared to those who did not, expected to delay that child's birth. While the earlier generation we surveyed planned to give birth toward the start of their career trajectories, the current generation is choosing to establish their careers and then downshift into childbearing. This delay in motherhood is particularly pronounced in those worried about holding down a job. Having children further into a career seems to them to be a less risky plan.

Raised for the most part in dual-career homes, Millennials have a realistic view of how difficult it can be to give one's all at work and at home.[35] One 2012 grad put this in sharp relief:

> *I'm going to go out on a limb, I don't know how many other girls would say this, but I would love to have a family. I would love to be able to create that nuclear unit that sometimes gets lost a little bit in the corporate culture. I have some friends…who are engaged or who are already getting married, which is baffling to me because, among my Wharton friends, we don't talk about these things. We're talking about how next year we're going to be on the road!*

—Female, Class of 2012

Summing Up

- Today's career-minded young women have separated esteem for motherhood from plans to actually become mothers.
- For women in 1992, motherhood fulfilled the need to help others. For women now, helping others means generating social impact through a successful career.
- Women are increasingly finding social fulfillment through networks of friends.
- Women's plans for whether to become mothers are linked to their choices about health and religion, which shows that they no longer feel obligated to have children as a way of satisfying preordained expectations.
- Young women today who plan to have children are more likely than those from a generation ago to delay doing so because of financial considerations.

CHAPTER 4

Redefining Family

We are in the midst of a revolution in gender roles, both at work and at home—a transformation with profound effects. This chapter explores what we discovered about the dynamics of long-term relationships in light of the panoply of new options available to both men and women.

For today's young men and women, plans for family are shifting from a primary focus on children. People place greater emphasis now on long-term relationships, friends, and extended friendship and job networks. Having a family and being a parent are no longer synonymous. Even though the idea of being a parent remains highly valued for the 2012 grads, plans for actually becoming a parent have drastically declined: We saw in 1992 that, for women, the more important they said parenting and long-term relationships were to them, the more likely they were to plan to have children. For women in 2012, this connection between their values and intentions no longer held.

Indeed, many of those we surveyed in 2012 were anticipating the creation of families that do not include children at all. Work and family responsibilities look different to those just embarking on adulthood's journey now than they did to the men and women who graduated a generation ago. Men and women are cultivating new models, characterized by an increasingly shared understanding of what it takes to fully experience the richness of work and family life. Before exploring the nature of these models, let's see what we observed about how things have changed with respect to the timing of children and expectations about time away from work for child care.

Timing of Long-Term Relationships and Children

Financial and career concerns shape plans for the timing of long-term relationships and children. One way Millennials have adjusted to the multiple challenges they face is to move such milestones further out. In our study, the age at which respondents expected to enter into a permanent relationship was higher for the Class of 2012. Following this trend, members of the Class of 2012 expected to be significantly older than members of the Class of 1992 (by about 1.5 years) at the time of the birth or adoption of their children.

In discussing their future family plans, graduates in 2012 saw no rush. Instead, they emphasized building a career first and diving into family life later, if at all. One young woman described her plan this way:

> For the next ten years, maybe work in consulting, get a law degree, go back to consulting or a company, and try and make a positive impact there. At twenty-eight or twenty-nine, I'd probably choose going toward the thing that will enrich me personally. Right now, if the choice is between something professional and a boyfriend, I would definitely choose the professional opportunity. But I don't want to be that person that's thirty-five and achieved a lot but doesn't have a family.

—Female, Class of 2012

A male classmate had a similar approach:

> Put the time into your career while you're young. Don't be in a big hurry to get married and have kids. It's great if you want to do those things, but you have time. If you plan to keep working after you start a family, it's important to have a well-established career first. It will be much easier to have a good work-life balance if you've already proven yourself in your career.

—Male, Class of 2012

Time Off

There's also the issue of how much time, in a competitive business environment, a new parent can afford (or wants) to take off from his or her career just after children arrive. In our study, among those who plan to have children, young people in 2012 expected to take less time off than did their 1992 counterparts. For example, among 1992 graduates who planned to take time off following the birth of their youngest child, 46 percent planned to take off six weeks or more; for 2012 graduates, this number was only 21 percent. This decrease in planned time off was seen in both men and women.

Women still plan to take more time off for child care than their male peers, and this gap did not change significantly between 1992 and 2012. Among 1992 respondents planning to take time off for their youngest child, only 13 percent of men expected to take off six weeks or more, compared to 81 percent of women. For 2012 participants, these numbers were lower but contained a similar gender gap—7 percent of men and 42 percent of women planned at least six weeks of leave.[36] Although both men and women plan to return to work sooner, women continue to bear the greater burden for childcare responsibilities.

But it's not just the length of parental leave that's shrinking—the proportion of young people expecting to take time off for childrearing has also fallen over the past 20 years. In 1992, 39 percent of graduates planned to take at least some time off after the birth of their youngest child; in 2012, this number was just 26 percent. This trend has been caused almost exclusively by changes in women's plans. In both cohorts, roughly one-fifth of men planned to take time off for their youngest child. But there is a big generational gap for women: while 69 percent planned to take time off for their youngest child in 1992, only 39 percent did so in 2012. Today, the majority of young women planning to become mothers are at least contemplating taking no time off after the birth of a child.

It's hard to say whether this reflects a choice to "lean in" to one's career or instead is a reflection of the perhaps unwanted demand to be present. With prominent female business leaders taking brief maternity leaves—including Yahoo! CEO Marissa Mayer, who famously took only two weeks off after having a son last year—young women seem to feel the need to minimize gaps in employment. Mayer's example reflects the ever-accelerating pace of business. As one young woman in the Class of 2012 put it:

The smallest amount of time that a woman could take off for a pregnancy or a birth, even the shortest amount of time, is going to have an impact. Because in the business world everything moves so fast that literally if you even miss a month, so much could happen in that month. I mean, careers are changed within months.

—Female, Class of 2012

The Ties That Bind

As we've emphasized throughout this book, the young people we studied aren't abandoning the concept of family. Rather, they are looking for (and finding) it in different places, including the families that are right under their noses. We found that today's men and women are more attached to their families of origin (parents, siblings, grandparents, aunts, uncles, and cousins) than were those in the Class of 1992. They were more likely than those in 1992 to report that their family of origin was a major source of satisfaction in their lives and that most of the important things that happen to them involve the family from which they came.

For both Gen Xers and Millennials, this attachment was greater among women than men. Nearly half the women (48 percent) we surveyed in 2012 said they were very involved in their families of origin, compared to 35 percent of the men. As one put it:

*The most significant influence on my life would have to be
my family. Growing up, they definitely shaped my values, my
aspirations. My parents had a big part. They were very involved
in my life.*

—Female, Class of 2012

Many of her classmates said much the same. Again, it may well
be a matter of economics. As the costs associated with education
have risen, and as the job market has taken a turn for the worse,
more young people have had to remain dependent on their parents
for financial support, and of course many of them boomerang
and return home. But this attachment to families of origin is also
linked to the delayed onset of adulthood today, which itself has a
significant financial component.[37] As mentioned previously, young
people are pushing back the ages at which they enter into permanent
relationships and, if they plan for children, at which they become
parents.

Converging Attitudes

As ideas about the structure of families are reimagined by today's
young men and women, there has also been a convergence of
attitudes about how to fashion long-term relationships in which
both partners have careers.

In 1992, women tended to believe that a dual-career relationship
works best with both parties equally involved in their work, equally
advanced in their careers, and with both careers having equal priority;
in other words, they aspired to equality. Their male classmates did
not share this same devotion to an egalitarian vision; they believed
that their wives' careers would be secondary to their own. But by
2012, men and women had converged to the point where their views
in these three areas were now alike.

Whereas today's men now have more egalitarian views than those in 1992, women's perspectives, by contrast, have shifted in the opposite direction. By 2012, they were no longer as sanguine about prospects for an equally shared, 50/50 commitment of time and attention to home and career. Compared to their counterparts in 1992, more women now are inclined to believe that dual-career relationships work best if one partner is less involved in his or her career.

Millennial men who hold more egalitarian views anticipate taking more time off after the birth of their children. This suggests that men who hold these egalitarian views—which are new for men—expect to live out their values in their future family lives.

When we asked whether both partners should agree on whose career has priority, the gender gap that was evident in 1992 had disappeared among 2012 respondents, with more women than in 1992 holding the view that one career should indeed take precedence over the other. With the way our question was worded, we don't know for certain which partner, but we do know this: Millennial women who said that two-career relationships work best when both partners agree on whose career has priority were more likely to rate (in a separate question) their *partner's* career as more important than their own. While more Millennial men are eschewing traditional gender roles, more Millennial women are reverting to them, with both genders' views meeting in the middle.

We also asked whether one partner should work part time or stay home to take care of the pair's young children. In 1992 this question yielded a significant gender gap, with men much more likely than women to say that, indeed, one parent should be home with young children. By 2012, this imbalance, too, had disappeared, and the convergence was due mainly to many fewer men believing that one partner should cut back on his or her career to care for children. Again, men are now more inclined than in the past to see the value of shared domestic responsibilities.

Yet many classic gender role differences still remain. Compared to men, women from both 1992 and 2012 were:

- Less likely to prioritize their own careers over those of their partners
- More likely to agree that two-career relationships work best when both partners understand the time their partner devotes to pursuing career goals
- More likely to agree that two-career relationships work best when there is agreement about how to take care of the children
- More likely to agree that two-career relationships work best when both partners share housework and childcare responsibilities
- More likely to expect their future partners to be employed in the long run

Young women we surveyed in 2012 were significantly more likely than their 1992 counterparts to accept a certain level of career inequality as the price of successful relationships. And this shift in women's thinking extends beyond careers.

We asked, for example, whether two-career relationships work best when both partners share responsibility for housework and child care and when neither partner has stereotypical or traditional views about family roles. While more women than men agreed with these views in both generations, women's agreement fell significantly over time, while there was no difference between Gen X and Millennial men. Today's women graduates are not expecting as much from their spouses on the domestic front as did their 1992 counterparts.

Leaning Back

This quote is typical of the women I interviewed:

This idea of growing up and having to figure out whether career is the most important thing or family—especially as a woman, I feel like I might have to make a decision at some point that I don't necessarily want to make.

—*Female, Class of 2012*

Almost to a person, women in the Class of 2012 were more aware than their peers from two decades earlier of having to choose between meaningful careers and long-term relationships in their lives. We asked survey respondents in both cohorts whether they agreed with this statement: "The conflicting demands of career and family will require that I decide which is more important." Sixty-one percent of women in 2012 agreed with this statement, significantly more than did women in 1992. And, in both 1992 and 2012, those women who said they would have to choose also tended to agree that two-career relationships work best when one partner is less involved in his or her career, when one partner is more advanced in his or her career, and when both partners agree on whose career has priority.

This apparent reversion to a more traditional mind-set is, like so much else, at least in part economically motivated. Women in 2012 who were more concerned about money matters were more likely to hold less egalitarian views about two-career relationships. For women in 2012, as opposed to those of 1992:

- The more they cared about earning a great deal of money, the more they agreed that one partner needs to be less involved in his or her career and that one partner should stay at home or work part time when the kids are young. (Indeed, in 1992 we saw the opposite: women then who were more concerned with high-paying careers were significantly less likely to think that one partner should scale back for children.)
- The more they cared about having a high standard of living, the more they believed that two-career relationships work best when one partner is less involved and less advanced in his or her career.

- The more they cared about material wealth, the more they thought that partners needed to agree on whose career had priority and that one partner should scale back his or her career for children.

Faced with today's economic pressures, young women anticipate having to make sacrifices in their careers so that their partners can earn lots of money and provide a high standard of living for their families. Even if they might prefer not to do so, Millennial women seem willing, at least for a time, to take a backseat for the sake of the financial gains earned by their partners.

Millennial women seem to be indicating that something has to give. It's as though they've thrown off the rose-colored glasses the previous generation wore. In 2012 we asked people whether they felt ready to make decisions that would allow them to stay true to their values. Those women who believed that one partner needed to be less involved in his or her career said they were less prepared to enact their values. In other words, they care about their careers and they care about starting families, but they cannot find a way, given current circumstances, to make both work.

Time required by work is yet another factor compelling women to believe that they must choose. Unlike their 1992 counterparts, those women in 2012 who anticipated having to work long hours in order to be successful were more likely to feel that they would be forced to decide whether career or family was more important. And they were more likely to agree that being a parent would limit their career success. For them, longer work hours seemed to mean decreased ability to achieve in both the professional and personal spheres. In 1992 just the opposite was true: Gen X women who expected longer work weeks were more likely to believe they would be able to "have it all."

Convinced they won't be able to excel both at work and at home, some women are giving up on creating a family with children, while others are preparing to make professional sacrifices for motherhood—sacrifices that the women of the Class of 1992 were not contemplating at the time of their graduation in their early twenties. We asked both generations, "How would you describe your current career priority relative to that of your partner?" Answer options ranged from "My career has a much higher priority than my partner's" to "Our careers have equal priority" to "My partner's career has a much higher priority than mine." In 1992, women who said that they definitely planned to have children saw their own careers as slightly more important than their partner's. In 2012, however, women who definitely planned to have kids saw their own careers as slightly less important than their partner's. Again, they were reporting that they believed they needed to choose; they did not readily see a clear path to having rich work and family lives that included children.

Women in 2012 who particularly valued careers that allowed time for family were more likely to expect their salaries 10 years after graduation, and in their first jobs, to be relatively low compared to their Wharton peers. In 1992, the opposite was true for first-job salaries. That is, women who cared about having time for their families were more likely to expect to earn more than their peers. Here, again, we see young women today who want family-friendly careers expecting that they will have to take a pay cut. Even in their first year in the workforce, they are anticipating the financial hit that family life will have on their careers.

Because the Millennials are a more recent generation, with more liberal attitudes—2012 students identified themselves as more liberal politically than their 1992 counterparts—we would expect that this younger cohort might hold more egalitarian beliefs. But as others have documented, gender roles are slow to change.[38] As in the past, the men and women in our sample overwhelmingly agreed that it is easier for men than for women to "have it all."

A Clearer View of What's Coming

Today's young, upwardly mobile college graduates, men and women, are more aware than their 1992 counterparts of what they are facing as they contemplate the road ahead. Women today know that inequalities exist, but they are reporting that they expect to bow to these pressures and accept accommodations. As one 2012 woman told me:

> *I don't want to sacrifice my career, but I think that down the line there has to be a balance—you know, I only have 24 hours in a day and I don't think I can do everything either. So, I don't know if there is a distinct tension between raising a family and managing your career, but I do think that at one point I'll have to try to see what my external circumstances are and then ask, "How do I make that choice?"*

—*Female, Class of 2012*

We do not yet have parity. Modern Parenthood, a 2013 study by the Pew Research Center, found that among dual-career couples with children, men and women performed roughly equal amounts of work, but dual-income fathers spent nearly 11 more hours per week in paid work than did mothers, who devoted more time to child care and housework than their partners. Fathers also enjoyed about 4.5 more hours of leisure time than mothers each week. The 2012 women in our study are well aware of these gaps, more so than those in 1992. As social commentator Lisa Belkin wrote in *The Huffington Post*:

> *Women educated during the '80s and early '90s—the women that the "Opt-Out Revolution" was about—never talked about limits and constraints in their college dorm rooms, they only talked of achievement. [Now] on campuses…they do talk about life and work. Not yet 21, they have devoured Anne-Marie Slaughter's Atlantic essay.*[39]

Today's young women have seen firsthand the hardships that lie ahead—through internships, through other work experience, and often within their own family circle. One 2012 graduate told me about a summer job she had working with a managing director of a major financial firm:

> *She had four children. They were all very young, and she'd been in banking for twenty years. But on a Friday night, she had to go into the office and do some work, and I was there working, and she had all these kids with her, and they were tired. They wanted to go home; they didn't want to be in the office. But she gave them a few toys just because she had to get her work done, and I think it sort of spoke to me that if you want both to be a very successful professional and have that rich family life, you may have to make sacrifices along the way.*
>
> *—Female, Class of 2012*

Part of the problem may be that, for all their greater awareness of the conflict between work and life, for all they've read about women opting out,[40] women have not gained ready access to successful role models[41]—though, with high-profile leaders such as Sheryl Sandberg and Anne-Marie Slaughter speaking out, this is quickly changing.

Today's women may also have sharper, more realistic views about the need for future sacrifices because of what *New York Times* editorial writer David Brooks calls a return to empiricism. In a 2013 column entitled "The Empirical Kids," Brooks argued that Millennials—who grew up witnessing 9/11, failed foreign interventions, the financial crisis, and fears about America's status as a global leader—are dismissing fuzzy, idealistic viewpoints in favor of a more cynical view about the future. For 2012 women in particular, this might mean replacing plans for an equitable future with some mix of resignation and realism as a way of coming to terms with either a future without children or one that consigns men and women to traditional gender roles.

So perhaps it's not really a matter of choice. While some consider that Gen X women who leave the workforce are opting out of their own volition, others—for example, Karen Kornbluh, former ambassador to the Organisation for Economic Co-operation and Development—differ: "I wouldn't call it a 'choice' in the classic sense," says Kornbluh, "because I don't think [women] have a lot of options. You're expected to give 100 percent on the home front and 100 percent at the work front and 100 percent to your friends and your community and you feel like a complete failure."[42] Then is it really a matter of choice that Millennials are opting out of parenthood?

Young women today are more informed about the limitations they face, including the stories of those before them and the reality that children need their parents' attention. At the same time, they have greater freedom in making the tough decisions they see ahead. There is no longer the kneejerk expectation of motherhood, of a mindless march into a predetermined future; nor are they looking through rose-colored glasses. And as we shall see, these young women also have the benefit of more support in their domestic relationships with men and, increasingly, at work, for making conscious and deliberate decisions about the lives they want to lead, in light of the barriers they know they face.

The New Knight in Shining Armor

Men have become more egalitarian—many more than in the past believe in the benefits of a 50/50 world—and particularly on a subject that used to divide the sexes sharply: working motherhood. Indeed, this shift in men's attitudes has been so great that it has eliminated the gap between men's and women's views on working moms.

Our study shows that men today are significantly less likely than their peers a generation back to think that children whose mothers are employed suffer because their mothers are not there when the children need them. While men were more likely than women to hold this position in 1992, in 2012 there was no difference between men and women on this question. Further, men in 1992 were more likely than women to think that one partner should ramp off the career track for the sake of children, but there is no longer a gender gap on this issue because fewer men subscribe to this point of view.

Millennial men have embraced the idea that women are in the workforce and that the kids will be all right. The new cultural hero for modern women who want to have children might well be the dad who "leans in" at home. As one 2012 man put it, when I asked if he would consider being a stay-at-home dad:

> *Since family is such a priority for me, I think it only makes sense for me to be open to the idea and consider it. It's just a matter of my being—I don't know what the word is—brave enough, confident enough to realize that family is the thing that is the most important to me. And so if that's my priority and my love, why would I not be the primary caregiver?*

> *—Male, Class of 2012*

Perhaps this kind of hero will be found more frequently in the stories young girls and boys hear at bedtime. Sandberg, Slaughter, and other women leaders—such as Xerox CEO Ursula Burns—urge young women to consider that their most important career choice is the husband they select.

Now to fill out the picture of the new egalitarian man, let's return to a subject I addressed earlier—Millennials' desire to have a positive social impact. We saw that in 2012, women who want to help others through their work perceive family life as a constraint on that goal. With men today, however, it's a very different story—the opposite, really. Millennial men for whom helping others is a substantial career interest are less likely to agree that one partner's career should take priority and are more likely to think that having an employed mother prepares children to be independent and able to do things on their own.

Further, to the extent that helping others is a crucial factor in defining their success in life, men today are more likely to believe that both partners should share responsibility for housework and child care, both partners should compromise, and neither partner should hold gender-stereotypical views about men's and women's family roles. Indeed, the 2012 men who said that neither partner should hold stereotypical ideas about gender roles were likely to value flexible work hours. They get it: they need to carry their weight at home.

In 1992, men who valued helping others also expressed more egalitarian beliefs about gender roles. What's new is that while men's inclination toward altruism, working toward social good, always meant providing more help for women, it now also translates into a greater capacity for men to manage the competing work and family domains of their own lives. Millennial men who valued helping others were less likely to predict that a demanding career would make it difficult to be an attentive partner and that they would have to make sacrifices in their family life to be successful at work.

The challenges of integrating work and family that lie before ambitious young men and women today are spawning new understandings of what a family can be. How we can all help find useful solutions that make sense for men and women of all ages, no matter what they take "family" to mean, is the topic we take up next.

Summing Up

- Millennials are adjusting to conflicts between work and family by moving milestones further out, including the age at which they expect to have children, if they expect to do so at all.
- For Millennials, "family" increasingly means networks of friends and a larger emphasis on family of origin, in part due to financial considerations.

- Women today are more aware of the challenges ahead of them and are structuring their relationships and careers accordingly.
- Women's hopes for and expectations of equitable sharing on the work and home fronts are on the wane: women today believe that something has to give, even if that means slipping back into more traditional roles.
- Men, meanwhile, are moving in the opposite direction. With them, egalitarianism is on the rise, especially in terms of beliefs about working motherhood.
- Today's men are in some ways similar to the women of 1992. They are optimistic about the prospect of both partners having thriving careers and sharing in the joys and struggles of living lives rich with friends and "family," however defined. And new models are being invented as I write.

CHAPTER 5

We Are All Part of the Revolution

The context for major life decisions about careers and families has changed for young business professionals. Men and women are much less inclined to plan to have children. Indeed, the very idea of family has shifted. Now let's try to make sense of our study's key findings and draw some practical implications for where we need to go from here—as a society, in our organizations, as individuals, and in our families—in the midst of what surely is a time of revolutionary change in gender roles, family structure, and career paths.

Is the Baby Bust a Good Thing or a Bad Thing?

I am not a population demographer or an expert in fertility planning; nor am I prepared to make moral judgments on the personal decisions of others. Demographers, economists, and historians are writing intelligently about the potential effects of the baby bust on the environment, the economy, health care, the military, and more.[43] What I can try to address is this: What do the radical shifts in young people's values and aspirations about careers and family life tell us about what we need to do to ensure a brighter future for them and for subsequent generations?

There are a few imperatives on which I don't think many will disagree: We need to continue replacing the human population, and children will still need caretakers to lovingly attend to them, educate them, and support them, both financially and emotionally, as they grow. We must continue to build a society that is ripe with opportunity and choice for both men and women. And for those people who want to become parents, it behooves us as a society to make it easy enough for them to foresee how they can realize this wish. We need our organizations and social institutions to cultivate an increasingly adaptable and productive workforce that can both compete in the global economy and raise the next generation.

Our current capacity to meet these challenges is cause for serious concern. Yet there are reasons for hope, too. We observed that young people are not including children in their future plans for a complex web of reasons. So there is no one solution; partial answers must come from various quarters. In this chapter, I'll offer recommendations based on what we found and what others have learned. I'll begin with ideas for action in social policy and education, and then describe what organizations can do. I'll next describe a model for empowering individuals to create sustainable change, with a particular emphasis on the challenges and opportunities faced by men who are aiming to lean in at home and win in their careers, as so much is already written by, for, and about women. I'll close with a few thoughts about new conceptions of family life. But first, a quick review of our major findings.

Highlights of What We Discovered

We found evidence of increased freedom and possibility as both men and women feel less constrained by gender role stereotypes. But we also observed significant challenges for Millennials who value parenthood but don't see a clear path toward it.

The Millennials in our study reported that work is consuming more and more of life. And both their family and career aspirations were lower than those of their Gen X counterparts. They described pressure to conform to a narrow set of career paths, a finding that runs counter to what's being observed in the careers of MBA students,[44] who are moving toward entrepreneurial ventures. I suspect that this shift among MBAs is in part a reaction to the limited options for meaningful and flexible work that many young people encounter in the standard post-undergraduate tracks. By their late twenties, young adults may come to realize that they want something more from their careers and they are able to assume greater control over their decisions than they had when they were 22.[45]

We observed, as others have,[46] the constraining effects of economic pressures on whether to have children (for men) and when to have them (for women). We also saw that men's plans for having children are shaped by their anticipation of future conflicts between work and family life, and that as their expectations of such conflicts have grown over these past two decades, their family ambitions have plummeted.

At the same time, we found that today's young people, and especially women, more so than in the past, planned to invest their energy in the social sphere, by addressing societal problems and by forming networks of friends and fellow professionals. While young women continue to value parenthood, many are expecting to find fulfillment through other means than motherhood. Young women who highly valued their health were disinclined toward parenthood. And the increasing proportion of women identifying as agnostic is another factor linked to reduction in plans for children. Further, young women now expect to be respected, want more time for their personal lives, and are more knowledgeable about what it takes to advance in their lives beyond the home. All told, there is a greater freedom for women to pursue paths that are uniquely meaningful to them, ones not prescribed by tradition or inherited norms. They're not locked into motherhood and seem better prepared now to forge their own paths.

Yet women we surveyed in 2012 were also more willing to accept either unequal career involvement in their relationships with life partners or no children at all because, as a number of them reported, they are aware (more than their Gen X counterparts seemed to have been) that someone needs to be with children when they are young. While much has been written about Gen X women opting out of their careers, we found that Millennial women are planning instead to opt out of motherhood. As many have decried, however, the so-called opting-out phenomenon may not actually be a choice, but rather an indication that we are providing neither the sustainable career pathways nor the childrearing supports women, and men, require to pursue rich and full work and family lives.

While gender-stereotypical differences between women and men about family and dual-career relationships persist, today's young men expect to see women as peers in the workforce, see engaged fatherhood as a way of contributing to society, and are increasingly cognizant of the impending difficulties in resolving conflicts between work and family life. They want flexibility as much as or more than women do.[47] Men's new awareness of and interest in the fullness of family life is a boon to women and children both.

Our study showed that men and women are now more aligned about how to decide who in a dual-career relationship should "lean in" to their careers and when they should do so. And because they expect greater parity in career opportunities and commitments, Millennial men are increasingly motivated to experiment with new models for how both partners can have more of what each wants in life. Indeed I could write an entire book, with new material cropping up daily, about the young, highly educated men who are writing about being stay-at-home-dads or about their experiences with paternity leave. Twenty years ago there was wide divergence between men and women; now there's more agreement about what it takes to make long-term relationships work. This convergence of attitudes promises greater collaboration and mutual support.

So, what does all this mean for what we should do now?

Strengthening the Infrastructure of Support through Social Policy and Education

As a commonwealth, we need to focus on what children in our society need: nurturing. How can they get it if the new norm is that both parents work and that we, unlike other developed countries and even many in the developing world, do not provide governmental and social supports for families? At present our government spends less and less on our children.[48] Our social policies must evolve to catch up to new realities: Women are in the workforce outside the home, men are conflicted about how to have rewarding careers and rich family lives, and children—"the unseen stakeholders"[49] at work—still need love and attention to thrive. Student debt is crushing the dreams of too many young people. They need relief from the astronomical and unsustainable cost of higher education. Our nation's youth are eager to serve society, but we don't provide a structure with incentives for national service. Indeed, those who want to pursue socially significant work anticipate that they will not be well remunerated; we as a society are not valuing service. What follows are actions we can and should pursue now.

Provide World-Class Child Care

Children require care, yet the United States continues to rank among the lowest in the developed world in the quality of the early childhood care we provide. Just as bad, the K–12 education we offer also falls short of our aspirations and of global norms. A massive overhaul could start with labor market compensation practices, which are now based on the principle that the younger the people a worker serves, the lower his or her pay. A more forward-thinking approach would be to reduce this ratio, with all the training and licensing requirements that would be needed to justify much higher rates of pay for those who care for our youngest citizens, arguably our most precious resource. Although this has not been a panacea in European countries, it does support the desires of our young people to become parents and also have careers.

Make Family Leave Available

Family leave, including paternity, is essential for giving parents the support they need to care for their children. Right now, only

11 percent of U.S. employees receive paid family leave from their employers.[50] The one public policy that covers time off to care for new children, the Family and Medical Leave Act, laudable though it is, still excludes 40 percent of the workforce. And millions who are eligible and need leave don't take it, mainly because it's unpaid, but also because of the stigma and real-world negative consequences.

We need to expand who's eligible for FMLA and to make it affordable. Family and medical leave insurance funds such as the ones established in California and New Jersey, where employees pay a small amount into an insurance pool and can then draw wages while they're out on leave, would make a huge difference in the lives of parents and children.[51] Such laws alter the frames of reference for decisions about flexible work policies and practices, making them more normative and legitimate, and as researchers Shelley Correll, Joan Williams, and others have observed, this helps to reduce the flexibility stigma[52] I talk about later, under "Changing Organizations." Many Millennials value parenting but can't see how to make it work. Flexibility without penalty will help.

Revise the Education Calendar

The standard school day is based on an outdated schedule. Other industrial and Western countries have children in schools for longer days and for a greater part of the calendar year. This provides much-needed support for working parents and, of course, greater enrichment for our children. Again, the data from our 2012 sample indicated that though young people see parenting as important in their lives, they are struggling to envision how to realize this aspiration. This is another front on which the public sector can provide help.

Support Portable Health Care

Given the increasing rates of interfirm mobility in our labor markets and the rising costs of health care, working parents benefit greatly from health care policies and practices that don't punish them for taking time off or moving. The Affordable Care Act is a step in this direction. It will help families obtain needed care while avoiding crippling debt as both parents might now have to navigate careers in which they move from job to job. Our data revealed that if young people are to plan for children, they will need more support than they currently expect to receive.

Relieve Students of Burdensome Debt

Skyrocketing interest rates on student loans and the increasing cost of higher education result in debt burdens that are too onerous. Our findings indicated that too many young people simply can't envision a future in which they can afford to support children. This must be changed.

Require Public Service

The increasing emphasis on careerism doesn't mean that young people don't also want to do work that helps others. They do, despite their expectation that they will not be well compensated for it. But how do we as a society channel that enthusiasm and idealism? We could require a year of public service for post-secondary school youth, as is the case in some European countries. Professors of graduate students regularly observe that those who have served in the military (in the United States or abroad) are, as a rule, better organized, more serious about their studies, more conscious of their responsibilities as leaders, and generally better prepared to make decisions. Requiring some sort of service may improve our workforce and help all of us recalibrate what's really important.

Display a Variety of Role Models and Paths

This might be an antidote to our finding that career paths have narrowed because students believe they must earn money quickly and that only a few career paths offer that option. The more that boys and girls hear stories about the wide range of noble, and economically viable, roles they can play in society, the easier it will be for them to choose freely the roles they are best suited for and want to play as adults. Young adults would benefit from opportunities to explore as wide an array of career alternatives as possible.

Teach Young People How to Lead Their Lives

In both primary and secondary schools, boys and girls can be taught how to discover who they really want to be, and they can start to practice the skills they will need to fulfill their aspirations. In college, an increasing number of courses teach young men and women how to think about what's important and what success in life means to them; about their roles and responsibilities to society and in the different parts of their lives; and how to integrate them in creative ways, including how to harness the power of new technologies for communication while maintaining room in one's life for meaningful in-person interaction. Placing greater emphasis on such training would enable young people to make more informed choices and would likely strengthen their resolve and their success in pursuing their aspirations. We have seen that religion has become less important in the lives of these young people, but it has not yet been supplanted by another lens through which to view what really matters in life.

Changing Organizations

Frustration at not being able to pursue a career and a family—a condition many young people reported—may compel unfulfilled employees to leave an organization. This, too, has to change, and it can. Organizations have many possible routes for helping Millennials, as well as others, while adding to the bottom line. Smart organizations have already recognized that they benefit from doing so through increased productivity, engagement, health, and retention of talent.[53] The best interests of companies competing in the marketplace for talent are served by demonstrating a true embrace of work arrangements customized by and for each individual—Millennial or otherwise.[54]

Naturally it's easier for anyone to try something new if there are role models in the organization who've shown by example that there are various ways to succeed, if there's demonstrated commitment from top executives to trying new ways of contributing to the organization's goals while devoting real attention to the other parts of life, and if there are stories being told of others who are similarly engaged in experimenting with flexible means for achieving results.

Millennials want work with meaning, but they also want and need more flexibility—without which they can't imagine a rich life beyond work—and greater control over how they spend their time.[55] And they are not alone in these desires. Gen X women who have opted out are also calling for greater flexibility.[56] Others are as well.

Following are ideas for actions employers can take that embrace these realities and support employees' development as valued assets to businesses.

Set Clear Goals Pursued by Flexible Means

Establish clear and measurable goals and expectations and give as much flexibility as possible as to where, when, and how the work is conducted. Recognize that employees' compensation is not just in the paycheck but, especially for Millennials, also in the control of their time.[57]

Declare That It's Not for Women Only

We don't need more initiatives that serve only to ghettoize work and family considerations as "women's issues." Men may be even more affected by conflicts between work and family.[58] Frame nonwork needs and interests, and all other family arrangements, as affecting not only mothers, but also fathers, couples who don't have children, single people, and those living in other family structures.

Provide Support for Childcare

Organizations should offer both regularly scheduled and emergency backup care. More important, for all businesses to be able to afford it, private-sector leaders should encourage government sponsorship of excellent child care for all Americans, just as we have state-provided kindergarten and just as other first-world countries provide these types of family-friendly supports.

Make Work Meaningful

Connect work to valued social benefits, whether this means providing more direct feedback from customers and clients about the value of a firm's services or products, or undertaking other initiatives to serve some charitable aim.[59] Compared to the past, young people today want to have a positive social impact through their work.

As we've seen, young women who want jobs that will allow them to serve others are less likely to plan to have children. If their jobs were more fulfilling—that is, if they resulted in greater social impact and made more use of their talents—these women could pursue their career and social goals in one and the same role. They might not feel the need to split time between work and civic engagement, because working hard in their careers would mean progressing toward the goal of positive social impact. Being better able to pursue their career and social goals might give them room to have children, if they so desired. And of course, young women and young men are not the only ones who want meaningful work; we all do.[60]

Show How Children Can Benefit from Having Working Parents

As journalist Lisa Belkin pointed out in her *Huffington Post* piece, Millennial women have been inundated with messages about "opting out" and the difficulties of juggling career and family. What these conversations are missing out on is this: careers can enhance family life, and family life can enhance careers; there is a way to weave both into a rich, strong tapestry.[61] A focus on the positive spillover effects of working parenthood may mean that fewer women will feel they must choose between personal and professional success and fewer men will allow fears of work-family conflict to inhibit their plans for fatherhood.

Young people need more positive examples. They need to hear loud and clear about executives such as John Donahoe, CEO of eBay, who leaned back to share in the care of his children; or Richard Fairbank, CEO of Capital One, who had his young children go to afternoon kindergarten in order that they would be able to stay up late enough for him to see them, and who coached and played every sport in which his eight children participated, all while pursuing a high-powered career. We need to let ambitious young people know that Double Dutch (jumping two ropes at once) is not only possible, it's fun.

Learn to Manage Boundaries and Change the Culture of Overwork

We're still at the start of the digital age, and we're just beginning to learn how to harness the power of technology and live in a hyper-connected world. Many people, not just Millennials, feel overwhelmed, and they need help, which smart businesses can provide, mainly by experimenting with what forms of communication work best and for what purposes.

Young people in our study expected to work 14 more hours per week more than their 1992 counterparts, and they associated these longer work hours with greater conflict between work and life. How to break this cycle? Reduced hours would help to retain Millennials and allow them to live rich lives outside work.[62] One avenue is through regulation. Another is through the encouragement of norms about boundaries between work and the rest of life. In too many workplaces and industries, long hours are still seen as a badge of honor. Changing these traditions can be accelerated by such programs as those described by Harvard professor Leslie Perlow, which give teams the tools for organizing their work so that members can have predictable time off.[63] Then tell the stories of successful alternatives to the standard model to make a range of such alternatives legitimate and culturally acceptable. End the glorification of the work warrior. Of course, saner work hours are better for all employees, not just Millennials. They are not the only ones experiencing the strain of overwork.

Fight the Flexibility Stigma

Many organizations do provide "family-friendly" programs of one sort or another. Yet employees in nonstandard work arrangements aren't seen in the same way as those who are,[64] to the detriment of much-needed innovations in how, when, and where work is accomplished. Too often those who manage workplace policies designed to be friendly to families inform parents about eligible leaves, then directly or indirectly question their dedication and commitment to the firm when they take advantage of those policies. Sharing the stories, far and wide, of admirably successful alternatives to the standard track must be part of the solution. We must create new norms and fight the flexibility stigma. To this end, slow careers may be a significant part of the solution.

Slow Careers

The slow movement (applied most famously to food) is about appreciating the value of basic human needs for connection and reflective living. Three decades ago, in 1980, organizational psychologist Lotte Bailyn wrote about the "slow burn way to the top,"[65] the benefits of which include normalization of alternative career paths; specifically slowing down during prime childrearing years without career penalties, and then ramping up again as children mature. Employers should demonstrate that it's acceptable, even desirable, to off-ramp and then on-ramp—for young men and women during the childbearing years, for older workers when they need to care for aging parents, and for all workers who need to take time off for any number of reasons. By providing models and encouragement for alternatives paths[66]—and perhaps organizing work according to a series of projects than based on static positions—organizations can signal to employees that their job security is not affected by their having children. This is how we retain talented Millennials and experienced senior employees, and truly support our young families. Creating a variety of possible career paths is also a way of attacking the flexibility stigma.

Giving Individuals the Tools and Support to Choose the Lives They Want

Societal and organizational assistance is essential, but individuals, too, can be empowered and taught how to find solutions that work for them and also how to gain the support they need to achieve the lives they want to live. The central observation of our study is that not all young people today feel compelled to plan for children. For some, this represents an unfortunate constriction of their life goals— they want children but don't see how they can manage it. For others, not having children is what they truly want, at least at this phase of their lives, and thus represents a new liberation from outdated and constraining gender stereotypes.

In either case, it's critical that we focus on what can be done to help young people pursue their true interests with passion and confidence. If they are helped to see how they can realistically bring a sense of purpose to their careers and find the time, space, and support in their lives for all their aspirations, possibly including children, without having to suffer the unbearable conflict between work and the rest of their lives that many of them now foresee, then perhaps more of those who want to be a parent at some point will actually plan to become one.

Providing this kind of help begins with the recognition that one size cannot fit all. Solutions customized by and for individuals to meet their specific needs and interests must be the order of the day. Fortunately, there are proven methods now available that are applicable not only to the problems facing Millennials but for people at all life stages. Let me tell you about one such method.

In the 1990s the Wharton Work/Life Integration Project researched best practices for how people effectively pursue the ideal of aligning their actions with their values, in all parts of their lives. Out of this field research evolved three simple principles:

1. Clarify what's important to you—your values and vision.
2. Recognize and respect all domains of life—work, home, community, and self.
3. Continually experiment with how goals are achieved.

At Ford Motor, where I was head of leadership development between 1999 and 2001, we successfully implemented a systematic process, called Total Leadership, grounded in these principles. We designed a series of exercises that culminated in practical, individualized experiments designed to produce "four-way wins"— improved performance at work, at home, in the community, and for the private self (mind, body, spirit). Our goal was to help individuals overcome the fear and guilt that inhibited them from taking action to makes things better for themselves as individuals, *and* for their families, *and* for our business, *and* for their communities. There was no *or* in this equation; it was all *and*.

Here's how it works: You articulate your values and vision for the future and then identify the most important people in the different domains of your life. You clarify mutual expectations in dialogue with these stakeholders, strengthening trust in the process. You think like a scientist and design experiments intended to produce four-way wins. Then you implement a couple of these experiments, measure their impact in all four domains of life, and, finally, reflect on what was learned from trying something new.

The key is that for each experiment, there are consciously intended benefits at work, at home, in the community, and for the private self—and some way to measure progress toward these benefits in each of the four domains. This is different from standard flex-time approaches where you ask your employer to give you something you want.

The usual result of such experiments is that people shift some of their attention from work to other parts of their lives and—in what seems paradoxical—they see improved performance at work and in the other domains because of greater focus, with less distraction, on the people and projects that really matter. They feel a greater sense of meaning and purpose, greater support for pursuing goals that matter, and more optimism about the future. Whether or not the experiments succeed, after reflecting on what works and what doesn't, they generate insights about how to create change in their lives that is sustainable, because such changes are actively and intentionally planned to produce benefits for all the different stakeholders in all domains of life. The most critical outcome is greater confidence and competence in their ability to initiate positive change. There's a shift in how they think about what's possible. They are less afraid to try new ways to make it all work. This is why this model is not only sustainable, but also contagious! And because it's entirely individualized, it's applicable to any life circumstance; this is not just for Millennials.

With students (undergraduates, MBAs, and executives) and in a wide array of organizations since 2001, we have found that, when given the chance, people are eager to take up the challenging task of experimenting with new ways to braid together the strands of their lives. And they're able to muster the courage and support to do so because they believe that the purpose of their initiatives is to make things better not just for themselves, not just for their families and communities, but for their organizations, too. This not only helps them overcome fear and guilt, but also buffers them against the flexibility stigma, because experiments are undertaken with the intent of achieving demonstrably improved performance at work. This is neither a perk nor a favor the company is doling out. Just the opposite: it's a boon to firm performance.

This approach directly addresses the needs we observed in Millennials to have work that is meaningful, to lead social lives that are rich, and to have flexibility and control in weaving a coherent tapestry. And of course this isn't the only proven approach to have emerged in the past decade.[67]

So instead of first thinking about workplace flexibility as a program that one might want to somehow take advantage of, what is needed is a fundamentally different mind-set, with the individual asserting control and thinking, "This does not have to be a zero-sum game." The biggest hurdle to adopting this kind of method is the common construction "work/life balance." As I've been arguing for decades, this term is retrogressive because it compels one to think automatically about conflict and trade-offs rather than encouraging creative thinking about practical ways of making life better in all its different parts.

Men Leaning In at Home

Much has been written already about how to help women succeed at home and at work, but men must be as much a part of the story as women. That's why I'm devoting this section to men. However you slice it, it's essential to have men's partnership in creating new alternatives—whether as stay-at-home-dads, dads with extensive paternity leaves, or dads sharing care—and in increasing their ownership of domestic responsibilities.

My subversive mission in creating the Total Leadership model was to provide the language and tools that men could use to address directly their particular challenges in integrating work and the rest of life without feeling they were doing the "women's work" of "finding balance." This is critical still, especially in light of how, as we observed, gender role stereotypes linger in this period of transition.

The key words in this model were not *work/life, work/family,* and certainly not *balance,* but rather, *leadership, performance,* and driving change to produce *results*—words that convey the idea that this business is not for women only. And it worked. This language makes it easier for organizations to gain acceptance for using this approach to help people—men and women, at all career stages and all levels—learn what they can do personally to create meaningful, sustainable change that increases their productivity at work and their commitment to their work, and improves their lives beyond work.

Men today expect to make bigger contributions to their households than their fathers did,[68] and the anticipation of conflict between home and work has increased. Just as women need support from their organizations and their families to surmount the hurdles of fear and tradition that keep them from achieving, men, too, need help getting past the roadblocks that keep them from engaging more fully as caregivers and homemakers. Breaking the mold of deeply rooted gender stereotypes won't be easy, because men face substantial barriers at work, in their homes, in their communities, and inside their own heads.[69] But for their fulfillment, and for women to advance in the world of work, men must advance in the world of home. The good news is that when men find smart, creative ways to dive in at home, they also perform better at work.

Traditional gender stereotypes are prisons for men, too, and hold many men back from trying new approaches to work and family life.[70] Like women, men are penalized for requesting or enacting flexible schedules. Men may wonder, "What if I'm just not a good dad? What if I'm perceived by my friends as unmanly because I'm doing 'women's work'? What if my children see me as a poor role model because I'm not the breadwinner?" There is whole new industry of stay-at-home-dad (SAHD) bloggers; websites, books, and articles by and for SAHDs; and gatherings where they explore in nuanced and poignant detail what they are struggling with, and reveling in, as they try to weave a new fabric that combines breadwinning and caregiving.[71]

So how does a man garner the courage to act, despite these worries and real-world impediments, and get his boss and coworkers to encourage him to have breakfast with his family, leave work in time to pick up the kids at school, take a paternity leave, and be truly focused on his family when he's with them instead of constantly checking his digital device about work matters? How can a man ask for the help he needs to sustain his involvement with his family and his work? And how does he enlist his family to support him in taking a more active role at home so that they see it as a benefit, not a nuisance, to them? In short, how can we help empower men so that they can foresee both manageable and, indeed, rich family and work lives even in unsupportive work environments?

Here's some advice, guys. First, think about what really matters to you and figure out what's not working and what you wish you could do to ameliorate the situation. In what ways are you failing to act in accordance with your values? What if your spouse or partner is unhappy with your lack of engagement and availability? If you're a father, do you feel that you're missing out on your kids' childhoods? Are you distracted by work when you're with your friends or at home and distracted by concerns about your family when you're trying to work? Asking these kinds of questions often produces these kneejerk reactions:

- There is no solution that will work because my boss would never go for changes.
- I can't ask for something that's just for me and my family because it's selfish.

• I know I'm not happy, but I don't see how things can improve, short of my leaving the job.

To get to the next step, it helps to find a peer coach (or two)—someone preferably outside of your immediate work circle—to talk to about what you're thinking. I have never seen anyone voice a problem for which someone else, with a fresh perspective, could not find new ways of seeing possibilities for positive change.

Then talk to those who matter most to you about what they really expect of you, how you're doing, and what you could do better. More often than not, what we think others expect of us is greater than (or a bit different from) what they actually expect of us. For example, you might think that being at work until very late is seen by your coworkers as a sign of your commitment and great performance when it is actually viewed as an indication of your inefficiency—as in, "Why can't you get your work done faster so that you don't need to be here this long into the night?" Find out exactly what the people who matter most to you need from you. Once you know more about what's actually expected, you're ready for the next step.

Try an experiment, a small change for a brief period (a week or a month) and keep front of mind the benefits not to you—you will not forget those, I promise—but to key people at work and to people you care about in other parts of your life.[72] An experiment is time limited and has measurable outcomes. The proof will be in the pudding, and your colleagues, family, and friends will be the judges. Make it clear that after the agreed-upon duration, if the experiment is not working for them, then you will return to the status quo, or try something else. No one has anything to lose, and all have something to gain. More often than not, when approached with this goal—to make it a win for all concerned—people around you might surprise you with their reasonableness.

When you invest intelligently in being a better father, or a better friend, or a better marathoner, then you will see how this makes you more confident in your parenting skills, friendships, or your physical condition, for example. The increased confidence spills over into other spheres; you become less distracted at work, more energetic, and have a clearer focus on business and family results that matter. As you grow more confident, you become less anxious about what others might think of you as you do more at home or spend less time at the office. Although the interventions can be fairly simple, the results can be dramatic—productivity usually increases at work because you are happier and more focused on important results.

For employers, helping men be more active at home, helping all employees be able to engage in the things that matter most to them, makes good business sense. It's wise to encourage people to engage in dialogues with important stakeholders and to experiment with small changes that can enrich their families, enhance their engagement with their community, and improve their health— all while enhancing the bottom line. By making it easier for men, and women, to live more whole, fully integrated lives, employers indirectly contribute to paving the way for the women in their lives to give more of themselves to their work and careers. And, of course, children win, too. We as a society are all the beneficiaries.

Reimagining Family Life

I don't believe that companies should be in the fertility planning business, but they should care about their employees being happy, if only so they can be more productive and so the good ones don't quit. And while it is essential to consider what businesses can do, in the near term it will be difficult to come up with organizational changes that increase young people's willingness to become parents. Governmental policy changes can be glacial, and societal norms often evolve slowly.

For those who do want to have children, there is a growing literature that can inform families about how to thrive when both parents are engaged as breadwinner and caregiver.[73] Jessica DeGroot, for example, has led the ThirdPath Institute's research on models of shared care, providing tools, inspiring examples, and support for families committed to the egalitarian ideal.

Men and women today are more likely than the previous generation to share the same values about what it takes to make dual-career relationships work. One implication of this finding is that there is greater solidarity among men and women and therefore more flexibility about the roles both men and women can legitimately take in society. There is now a greater sense of shared responsibility for domestic life. Young men are realizing they have to do more at home than their fathers did, and today's young men want to do so. The Families and Work Institute's research on the "new male mystique" affirms this trend, as do Brad Harrington's New Dad research at the Boston Center for Working Families and Michael Kimmel's decades-long studies of masculinity.

Of course the sharing of care can happen either in series or in parallel, with costs and benefits linked to both options. A clear pattern we observed is that young people are forestalling the arrival of children. Perhaps this foretells a "slow family" movement to coincide with slow-burn careers—a variety of family life models that enable both partners, at different stages of their lives or simultaneously, to engage more or less, depending on their needs and interests, in their families and in their careers.

With more available and legitimate choices for family life, stronger support from organizations, wiser social policy, and greater confidence in their ability to create meaningful change, young men and women can flourish in all the roles that matter to them—at work, at home, and in their communities—in ways we've not yet seen.

Conclusion
An Invitation to Help Spur Cultural Change

The field of research and practice known as work/life is about advancing the cause of human liberation. It's dedicated to the idea that men and women can and must have freedom of choice in how they live, work, and contribute to making the world better for the generations to come. Work/life is a social movement to benefit the next generation—a field of study with powerful ideas for transforming business to make more humane and effective use of people and technology.

While it used to be that young women had aspirations for achievement that were lower than those of their male counterparts, today those aspirations are the same for both groups. With a more clear-eyed vision of what is to come—and with men and women holding more aligned views about the value of work and parenting— my hope is that people at all life stages will take more focused, concerted action to chip away at the established order and more successfully pursue new options.

But cultural change is a slog. It's messy, and it proceeds in fits and starts. Traditions and institutions, like people, tend to resist change; the diffusion of new ideas about social roles happens over long stretches of time. As our study and so many others have observed,[74] much tumult and confusion accompany our evolving grasp of the possibilities for men's and women's roles.

Still, we are at the cusp of the emergence of new models. Young people are increasingly active in consciously and deliberately crafting their roles. Attitudes are changing. Yes, it remains incredibly difficult for women to break through to the top strata, and yes, opting for the nontraditional path of stay-at-home-dad, even for short periods, remains challenging for men. But we are seeing more expressed freedom, more realistic goals, and more unity among young men and women as they create new ways to pursue lives that fit with who they truly want to be.

I see enormous opportunity at this moment in history for the work/life field to pave the way by describing as teachers and scientists, by demonstrating as innovative practitioners, by advocating as agents of social change, and by celebrating as leaders through the stories we can tell of the remarkable variety of successful solutions that people in all kinds of organizations—young and old, men and women, gay and straight, healthy and infirm, religious and agnostic—are discovering through creative, courageous experimentation in living and working.

By describing, demonstrating, advocating for, and celebrating these innovations, we increase understanding, visibility, and legitimacy of the possibilities, and so inspire new models to spring up and flourish. By making the strange seem normal and the weird apt, we can spur the cultural change we need to unshackle the millions constrained by outmoded stereotypes and narrow-minded expectations, enabling them to pursue with neither fear nor guilt the lives they truly want to lead.

Let's work together toward this aim.

For information about the activities of the Wharton Work/Life Integration Project since its founding in 1991, visit www.worklife .wharton.upenn.edu, where you can find descriptions of our research, teaching, conferences, and impact on practice and policy. Copies of the surveys used for this research and reports with basic statistical analyses are freely available there too. For information and materials on Total Leadership, which I created while serving as head of leadership development for Ford Motor (1999–2001) and which was influenced by the Work/Life Integration Project's efforts in the 1990s, visit www.totalleadership.org.

Acknowledgments

The Wharton School has been my professional home for nearly 30 years, and I am grateful for the support and encouragement of my colleagues and mentors there. From the start of his tenure as dean, Tom Gerrity has been a generous sponsor and advocate of my initiatives in both the work/life and leadership fields, providing the vision and resources needed to get both the Work/Life Integration Project and the Graduate and Undergraduate Leadership Programs off the ground. I am deeply appreciative for the backing and the faith that both he and Janice Bellace—first as vice dean for our Undergraduate Division and then as Wharton's deputy dean—had in me.

I am grateful for the financial contributions to the 1992 survey provided by University of Pennsylvania alumnus Robert Romanow (College of Arts and Sciences, Class of 1962), the Jerrold Fine Scholarship Fund, and the Jon Burnham Scholarship Fund. Many colleagues in the Management Department, and in other parts of Penn, have given me invaluable support over the years. I am grateful to Peter Cappelli, director of the Wharton Center for Human Resources, and to Mike Useem, director of the Center for Leadership and Change, for co-sponsoring this particular project. They provided critically important input, as did my colleagues Matthew Bidwell, Adam Cobb, Adam Grant, Ethan Mollick, and Amy Wrzesniewski, by reviewing, editing, and contributing questions to the follow-up survey of the Class of 1992 and to the survey of the Class of 2012. The original survey was informed by a project done in collaboration with my neighbors and friends at Drexel University, Jeff Greenhaus and Saroj Parasuraman, to whom I am very grateful. Thanks also to Ellen Galinsky, president of the Families and Work Institute, who contributed questions to the 2012 surveys, and to researchers

Alyssa Westring, of DePaul University, and Wendy Casper, of the University of Texas at Arlington, who did so as well. When I told Alyssa a few years ago that I was planning a follow-up with the Class of 1992, she said, "Why not survey the Class of 2012, too, as a point of comparison?" Thank you, Alyssa! Liza Law, and her colleagues in Wharton's Computing and Information Technology group, gave graciously of their time in helping to retrieve the 1992 data.

Throughout my career at Penn, I have had the enormous good fortune to teach and also to learn from a phenomenally talented group of undergraduate and graduate students. Twenty years ago, Jessica DeGroot (Wharton MBA, Class of 1994), while creating her own path in our MBA program, was my partner in launching the Work/Life Integration Project. On this follow-up study, Molly Reed (College of Arts and Sciences, Class of 2012) contributed her energy, deep insight, and incredibly high levels of technical skill to virtually all phases of the research, especially in the analysis and interpretation of our results. I am confident that she will achieve great heights as a scholar as she moves on to her doctoral studies. Sherry Yang (Wharton Undergraduate, Class of 2014) and Michelle Rajotte (Wharton MBA, Class of 2007) brought their care, dedication, and keen intellects to building the 2012 surveys, administering them, organizing and managing the data, and preparing reports for our study participants. Adam Kapelner and Justin Bleich, both doctoral students in the Statistics Department at Wharton, provided useful guidance on translating the antiquated 1992 data, building and cleaning the statistical database for both classes, and evaluating analytic models. Frank DelPizzo (Wharton Undergraduate, Class of 2015) and Hanna Kamaric (Wharton Undergraduate, Class of 2014) used their many talents to assist in the analysis and interpretation of our findings.

I am grateful to the 800 students in the Classes of 1992 and 2012 who gave generously of their time to complete the lengthy and personal surveys about their lives, values, and perspectives on work and family, politics, religion, and who made this information available for all of us. I am immensely grateful to them all, and especially to the 17 students who sat for a videotaped interview with me, for their commitment to our school and for their contribution to our search for useful knowledge. I'd like to thank Joseph Ansanelli and Joy Jakobovits Waters, the co-chairs of the Class of 1992's Dean's Undergraduate Student Advisory Board.

The ideas in this book were shaped by my reading and talking with the many scholars, journalists, and practitioners in the work/life field, to whom I am grateful for inspiring me and pushing my thinking, including Lotte Bailyn, Roger Brown, Ted Childs, Kathy Christensen, Perry Christensen, Dana Friedman, Ellen Galinsky, Tim Hall, Brad Harrington, Ellen Kossek, Jim Levine (a leading light in the field of fatherhood who, in his current role, also provided great counsel as my literary agent), Kathie Lingle, Sharon Lobel, Linda Mason, Leslie Perlow, Nancy Rothbard, and Sue Shellenbarger.

I am very grateful to have had the opportunity to work with the Wharton Digital Press team (later renamed Wharton School Press), led by my wise and constructively critical colleague Steve Kobrin. Shannon Berning and Howard Means were both razor-sharp and, at the same time, gentle editors, providing invaluable guidance and feedback on the manuscript and helping bring it to fruition.

Most important, I want to acknowledge and thank my family, without whom my work would be without meaning. My parents, Leah and Victor Friedman, and my siblings, Susan Schrott and Paul Ben-Victor, are a continued source of unconditional love and support, and for this I am most appreciative.

To my wife, research colleague, business partner, and best friend, Hallie, there are no words to capture the scope of my gratitude for making possible everything that is worthwhile in my life. As an accomplished clinician and scholar, whose dissertation focused on career transitions and their impact on family life, Hallie read, contributed to, and edited the manuscript. Her nuanced, incisive ideas about work and family life were invaluable. I am grateful to my eldest child, Gabriel, the one whose birth instigated a change in the direction of my career, for his very helpful critique of the manuscript from his perspective as a Millennial man; to my son Harry, for his genius IT support and general shenanigans; and to my daughter, Lody, for her unvarnished opinions about life as a Millennial woman, and about everything else. To all four I am grateful for enabling (in a good way) my work and making my life real.

Merion Station, August 2013

Notes

1 J. Chamie and B. Mirkin, "Childless by Choice: More People Decide against Having Children, Presenting Quandaries for Governments and the Elderly," *YaleGlobalOnline*, March 2, 2012, at http://yaleglobal.yale.edu/content/childless-choice; J. V. Last, *What to Expect When No One's Expecting: America's Coming Demographic Disaster* (New York: Encounter Books, 2013); D. S. Hoff, *The State and the Stork: The Population Debate and Policy Making in U.S. History* (Chicago: University of Chicago Press, 2012); and P. Longman, *The Empty Cradle: How Falling Birthrates Threaten World Prosperity and What to Do about It* (New York: New America Books, 2004).

2 T. Riley, "Average Debt Burden Highest of Ivies, Lowest in R.I.," *Brown Daily Herald*, November 7, 2012; and R. F. Elliott and K. R. Zavadski, "Graduating with Debt," *Harvard Crimson*, October 18, 2012.

3 M. Jackson, *Distracted: The Erosion of Attention and the Coming Dark Age* (Amherst, NY: Prometheus, 2008); and A. Ollier-Malaterre, N. Rothbard, and J. Berg, "When Worlds Collide in Cyberspace: How Boundary Work on Online Social Networks Impacts Professional Relationships," *Academy of Management Review* (2013), at doi:10.5465/amr.2011.0235.

4 T. Erickson, "Gen Y in the Workforce," *Harvard Business Review* (February 2009); K. Foster, *Generation, Discourse, and Social Change* (New York: Routledge, 2013); J. Gilbert, "The Millennials: A New Generation of Employees, A New Set of Engagement Policies," *Ivey Business Journal* (September–October 2011); H. Seligson, *Mission: Adulthood: How the 20-Somethings of Today Are Transforming Work, Love, and Life* (New York: Diversion Books, 2012); B. Ballenstedt, "Millennials Are Rewriting the Definition of Work," Nextgov, May 29, 2013; and S. Lyons, L. Duxbury, and C. Higgins, "An Empirical Assessment of Generational Differences in Basic Human Values," *Psychological Reports* 101 (2007): 339–52.

5 S. D. Friedman and J. H. Greenhaus, *Work and Family—Allies or Enemies? What Happens When Business Professions Confront Life Choices* (New York: Oxford University Press, 2000).

6 See, for example, Ellen Galinsky's work at the Families and Work Institute; Brad Harrington and Brad Googins's and others' work at the Center for Work and Family at Boston College; and Ellen Kossek's long stream of rigorous research, and the many other researchers cited in this book.

7 S. M. Bianchi, "Changing Families, Changing Workplaces," *Future of Children* 21, no. 2 (2011): 15–36.

8 Riley, "Average Debt Burden Highest of Ivies"; and Elliott and Zavadski, "Graduating with Debt."

9 M. Dillon, P. McCaskey, and E. Blazer, "MBA Internships: More Important Than Ever," *Journal of Education for Business* 86, no. 1 (2010): 44–49.

10 E. S. W. Ng, L. Schweitzer, and S. T. Lyons, "New Generation, Great Expectations: A Field Study of the Millennial Generation," *Journal of Business and Psychology* 25, no. 2 (2010): 281–92.

11 *Ibid.*

12 Twenge and others have found that recent generations display increased individualism, extroversion, self-esteem, and a decreased need for social approval. J. M. Twenge, W. K. Campbell, and E. C. Freeman, "Generational Differences in Young Adults' Life Goals, Concern for Others, and Civic Orientation, 1966–2009," *Journal of Personality and Social Psychology* 102, no. 5 (2012): 1045–62. Seligson and others emphasize the positives—how this generation is open-minded, civically engaged, and seeking personal fulfillment through doing meaningful work. H. Seligson, *Mission: Adulthood: How the 20-Somethings of Today Are Transforming Work, Love, and Life* (New York: Diversion Books, 2012).

13 S. Eisner, "E-employment? College Grad Career Building in a Changing and Electronic Age," *American Journal of Business Education* 3, no. 7 (2010): 25–40; and G. T. Chao and P. D. Gardner, "Today's Young Adults: Surfing for the Right Job," College Employment Research Institute, Michigan State University, 2007.

14 P. Cappelli, *Why Good People Can't Get Jobs: The Skills Gap and What Companies Can Do about It* (Philadelphia: Wharton Digital Press, 2012); R. Hoffman, B. Casnocha, and C. Yeh, "Tours of Duty: The New Employer-Employee Compact," *Harvard Business Review* (June 2013); and E. E. Kossek, M. Valcour, and P. Lirio, "The Sustainable Workforce: Organizational Strategies for Promoting Work-Life Balance and Well-Being," in C. Cooper, and P. Chen, eds., *Wellbeing in the Workplace: From Stress to Happiness* (Oxford, UK, and New York: Wiley-Blackwell, 2013).

15 H. Wolff and K. Moser, "Effects of Networking on Career Success: A Longitudinal Study," *Journal of Applied Psychology* 94, no. 1 (2009): 196–206.

16 S. A. Hewlett and C. B. Luce, "Extreme Jobs: The Dangerous Allure of the 70-Hour Workweek, *Harvard Business Review* 84, no. 12 (December 2006): 49–59.

17 J. M. Zauzmer, "Where We Stand: The Class of 2013 Senior Survey," *Harvard Crimson*, May 28, 2013.

18 S. Fuller, "Job Mobility and Wage Trajectories for Men and Women in the United States," *American Sociological Review* 73, no. 1 (2008): 158–83; and PricewaterhouseCoopers, *PwC's NextGen: A Global Generational Study*, 2013, at http://www.pwc.com/en_US/us/people-management/publications/assets /pwc-nextgen-summary-of-findings.pdf.

19 R. Franke, S. Ruiz, J. Sharkness, L. DeAngelo, and J. Pryor, "Findings from the 2009 Administration of the College Senior Survey (CSS): National Aggregates," 2010, at http://www.heri.ucla.edu/PDFs/pubs/Reports/2009_CSS_Report.pdf; Higher Education Research Institute, UCLA, "Class of 2012: Findings from the College Senior Survey," May 2013, at http://www.heri.ucla.edu/briefs /CSS2012-Brief.pdf; Higher Education Research Institute UCLA, CIRP. H. S. Astin and A. Antonio, "The Impact of College on Character Development," *New Directions for Institutional Research* 122 (2004): 55–64; and G. D. Kuh and P. D. Umbach, "College and Character: Insights from the National Survey of Student Engagement," *New Directions for Institutional Research* (2004): 37–54, at doi: 10.1002/ir.108.

20 Ng, Schweitzer, and Lyons, "New Generation, Great Expectations"; PwC, *PwC's NextGen*.

21 E. Galinsky, N. Carter, and J. T. Bond, *Leaders in a Global Economy: Finding the Fit for Top Talent* (New York: Families and Work Institute and Catalyst, 2008); Society for Human Resource Management, *2009 Employee Job Satisfaction: Understanding the Factors That Make Work Gratifying*, 2009, at http://www.shrm.org/research /surveyfindings/articles/documents/09-0282_emp_job_sat_survey_final.pdf.

22 Among all U.S. employees, the desire for greater responsibility decreased from 54 percent in 1992 to 40 percent in 2002. E. Galinsky, K. Aumann, and J. T. Bond, "Times Are Changing: Gender and Generation at Work and at Home," New York: Families and Work Institute, 2011, at http://familiesandwork.org/site/research /reports/Times_Are_Changing.pdf.

23 Other researchers are finding similar conflict between work and family life for young men. See, for example, K. Aumann, E. Galinsky, and K. Matos, *The New Male Mystique* (New York: Families and Work Institute and Catalyst, 2011); and K. Parker and W. Wang, "Modern Parenthood: Roles of Moms and Dads Converge as They Balance Work and Family," Pew Research Social and Demographic Trends, 2013, at http://www.pewsocialtrends.org/2013/03/14/modern-parenthood-roles-of-moms -and-dads-converge-as-they-balance-work-and-family/.

24 This supports evidence that the impact of maternal employment is minimal. S. Bianchi, "Maternal Employment and Time with Children: Dramatic Change or Surprising Continuity?" *Demography* 37, no. 4 (2000): 401–14.

25 Bianchi, "Changing Families, Changing Workplaces"; Galinsky, Aumann, and Bond, "Times Are Changing"; and Parker and Wang, "Modern Parenthood."

26 Gloria Goodale, "Behind the Falling US Birthrate: Too Much Student Debt to Afford Kids? *Christian Science Monitor*, January 30, 2013.

27 J. Stiglitz, "Student Debt and the Crushing of the American Dream," *New York Times*, May 12, 2013.

28 G. Livingston and D. Cohn, "Childlessness up among All Women; Down among Women with Advanced Degrees," Pew Research Social and Demographic Trends, 2010, at http://www.pewsocialtrends.org/2010/06/25/childlessness-up-among-all -women-down-among-women-with-advanced-degrees/.

29 K. Park, "Childlessness: Weber's Typology of Action and Motives of the Voluntarily Childless," *Sociological Inquiry* 75, no. 3 (2005): 372–402.

30 L. S. Scott, *Two Is Enough: A Couples' Guide to Living Childless by Choice* (Berkeley, CA: Seal Press, 2009).

31 F. Bruni, "Our Pulchritudinous Priesthood," *New York Times*, July 27, 2013.

32 Pew Research Center, "'Nones' on the Rise: One-in-Five Adults Have No Religious Affiliation," Pew Forum on Religion and Public Life Project, October 9, 2012, at http://www.pewforum.org/files/2012/10/NonesOnTheRise-full.pdf.

33 Similar findings: S. R. Hayford and S. P. Morgan, "Religiosity and Fertility in the United States: The Role of Fertility Intentions," *Social Forces* 86, no. 3 (2008): 1163–88.

34 Goodale, "Behind the Falling US Birthrate."

35 R. G. Cinamon, "Anticipated Work-Family Conflict: Effects of Gender, Self-Efficacy, and Family Background," *The Career Development Quarterly* 54 (2006): 202–15.

36 Millennial men in our study appear to be following contemporary norms on paternal leave. F. V. Deusen, B. Harrington, and B. Humberd, *The New Dad: Caring, Committed, and Conflicted* (Chestnut Hill, MA: Boston College Center for Work and Family, 2011).

37 J. J. Arnett, "Emerging Adulthood(s): The Cultural Psychology of a New Life Stage," in L. A. Jensen, ed., *Bridging Cultural and Developmental Approaches to Psychology: New Syntheses in Theory, Research, and Policy* (New York: Oxford University Press, 2011), pp. 255–57.

38 K. Gerson, *The Unfinished Revolution: Coming of Age in a New Era of Gender, Work, and Family* (New York: Oxford University Press, 2010).

39 "The Retro Wife Opts Out: What Has Changed and What Still Needs To," *Huffington Post*, March 19, 2013, at http://www.huffingtonpost.com/lisa-belkin/retro-wife-opt -out_b_2902315.html?utm_hp_ref=fb&src=sp&comm_ref=false#sb=2291676,b=fa cebook.

40 P. Stone, *Opting Out? Why Women Really Quit Careers and Head Home* (Berkeley: University of California Press, 2007).

41 Kelan, for example, has found that Millennial women are ambivalent about their female role models, using different words than men do to describe them. E. Kelan, *Rising Stars: Developing Millennial Women as Leaders* (New York: Palgrave Macmillan, 2012).

42 Kornbluh quoted in R. Madell, "Is There Really a Choice between Work and Family?" *The Glass Hammer*, April 10, 2013, at http://www.theglasshammer.com /news/2013/04/10/is-there-really-a-choice-between-work-and-family/.

43 Chamie and Mirkin, "Childless by Choice"; Last, *What to Expect When No One's Expecting*; Hoff, *The State and the Stork*; and Longman, *The Empty Cradle*.

44 E. Rowe, "More Wharton MBAs Are Opting for Startups," *BloombergNews*, June 25, 2013.

45 B. Williams, "The End of Careers as We Know Them: Lifelong and Full-Time Careers Are Disappearing," *Psychology Today*, July 11, 2013.

46 Elliott and Zavadski, "Graduating with Debt"; R. *Harvard Crimson*. Fry, "Young Adults After the Recession: Fewer Homes, Fewer Cars, Less Debt," Pew Research Social and Demographic Trends, February 21, 2013, at http://www.pewsocialtrends. org/files/2013/02/Financial_Milestones_of_Young_Adults_FINAL_2-19.pdf; Riley, "Average Debt Burden Highest of Ivies," and *The Brown Daily Herald*; and Stiglitz, "Student Debt and the Crushing of the American Dream."

47 Galinsky, Aumann, and Bond, *Times Are Changing*; M. Berelowitz and N. Ayala, "The State of Men, *JWT Intelligence* (June 2013), at http://www.jwtintelligence.com

/wp-content/uploads/2013/06/F_JWT_The-State-of-Men_Trend-Report_06.04.13.
pdf; A. Dembosky, "The Rise of Silicon Dad," *Financial Times*, April 19, 2013;
M. Fulcher and E. F. Coyle, "Breadwinner and Caregiver: A Cross-Sectional Analysis
of Children's and Emerging Adults' Visions of Their Future Family Roles," *British
Journal of Developmental Psychology* 29 (2011): 330–46; and Parker and Wang,
"Modern Parenthood."

48 D. Porter, "Pro-Baby, but Stingy with Money to Support Them," *New York Times*,
July 23, 2013; First Focus, *Children's Budget 2013*, Washington, DC, at http://www
.firstfocus.net/sites/default/files/ChildrensBudget2013.pdf.

49 The term Jeff Greenhaus and I use in *Work and Family—Allies or Enemies?*

50 L. Houser and T. P. Vartanian, *Pay Matters: The Positive Economic Impacts of Paid
Family Leave for Families, Businesses and the Public* (New Brunswick, NJ: Center
for Women and Work, School of Management and Labor Relations, Rutgers
University, 2012).

51 E. Appelbaum and R. Milkman, "Leaves That Pay: Employer and Worker
Experience with Paid Family Leave in California," Center for Economic and Policy
Research, 2011, at http://www.cepr.net/documents/publications/paid-family
-leave-1-2011.pdf.

52 J. Williams, S. Correll, J. Glass, and J. Berdahl, eds., "Special Issue: The Flexibility
Stigma," *Journal of Social Issues* 69, no. 2 (2013); C. Goldin and L. F. Katz, "The
Cost of Workplace Flexibility for High-Powered Professionals," *The Annals of the
American Academy of Political and Social Science* 638, no. 1 (2011): 45–67.

53 E. Galinsky, J. T. Bond, and E. J. Hill, *When Work Works: A Status Report on
Workplace Flexibility: Who Has It? Who Wants It? What Difference Does It Make?*
(New York: Families and Work Institute, 2004).

54 J. Blades and N. Fondas, *The Custom-Fit Workplace: Choose When, Where, and How
to Work and Boost Your Bottom Line* (Hoboken, NJ: Jossey-Bass, 2010).

55 See, for example, T. Erickson, "Gen Y in the Workforce," *Harvard Business Review*
(February 2009); K. Foster, *Generation, Discourse, and Social Change* (New York:
Routledge, 2013); L. Gratton, *The Shift: The Future of Work Is Already Here* (London:
HarperCollins, 2011); A. Maitland and P. Thompson, *Future Work: How Businesses
Can Adapt and Thrive in the New World of Work* (New York: Palgrave Macmillan,
2011); and Seligson, *Mission: Adulthood*.

56 Stone, *Opting Out*; and Gerson, *The Unfinished Revolution*.

57 Google famously grants employees a percentage of their paid work time to pursue their own projects; and Salesforce allows four hours per week or six days per year for volunteer work outside the company, on company time.

58 Galinsky, Aumann, and Bond, *Times Are Changing*; and Aumann, Galinsky, and Matos, *The New Male Mystique*.

59 A. M. Grant, "Leading with Meaning: Beneficiary Contact, Prosocial Impact, and the Performance Effects of Transformational Leadership," *Academy of Management Journal* 55 (2012): 458–76; and B. D. Rosso, K. H. Dekas, and A. Wrzesniewski, "On the Meaning of Work: A Theoretical Integration and Review," *Research in Organizational Behavior* 30 (2010): 91–127. See Warby Parker, *Neil Blumenthal: Secrets to Warby Parker's Rapid Growth*, at http://www.inc.com/neil-blumenthal /neil-blumenthal-warby-parker-secrets-to-rapid-growth.html.

60 C. Michaelson, M. G. Pratt, A. M. Grant, and C. P. Dunn, "Meaningful Work: Connecting Business Ethics and Organization Studies," *Journal of Business Ethics* (March 2013).

61 For example, a Pew study found that working mothers felt slightly better about their parenting than did nonworking mothers, and 78 percent of mothers who worked full or part time said they were doing an excellent or very good job as parents, whereas only 66 percent of nonemployed mothers said the same. Parker and Wang, "Modern Parenthood."

62 R. C. Barnett and D. T. Hall, "How to Use Reduced Hours to Win the War for Talent," *Organizational Dynamics* 29, no. 3 (2001): 192–210.

63 L. A. Perlow, *Sleeping with Your Smartphone* (Boston, MA: Harvard Business Review Press, 2012).

64 As Williams, Correll, Glass, and Berdahl, "Special Issue," point out.

65 L. Bailyn, "The 'Slow Burn' Way to the Top: Some Thoughts on the Early Years in Organizational Careers," in C. B. Derr, ed., *Work, Family, and the Career: New Frontiers in Theory and Research* (New York: Praeger, 1980).

66 M. Alboher, *The Encore Career Handbook: How to Make a Living and a Difference in the Second Half of Life* (New York: Workman, 2013); and K. Christensen, "Older Workers, Adult Children and Working Longer," *Huffington Post Business*, October 29, 2012.

67 For example, D. M. Rousseau, *I-deals: Idiosyncratic Deals Employees Bargain for Themselves* (Armonk, NY: M. E. Sharpe, Inc., 2005).

68 See http://www.bc.edu/content/bc/centers/cwf/news/TheNewDad.html; and Aumann, Galinsky, and Matos, *The New Male Mystique*.

69 J. A. Vandello, V. E. Hettinger, J. K. Bosson, and J. Siddiqi, "When Equal Isn't Really Equal: The Masculine Dilemma of Seeking Work Flexibility," *Journal of Social Issues* 69, no. 2 (2013): 303–21.

70 Gerson, *The Unfinished Revolution*.

71 For a few examples of blogs, articles, and books by young, highly educated men staying at home or sharing child care, see http://www.nycdadsgroup.com/; http://fathersworkandfamily.com/about/; http://dadoralive.com/; N. Brand, "Why I'm Not a Father," *The Good Men Project*, June 12, 2012, at http://goodmenproject.com/fathers-day/why-im-not-a-father/; R. Dorment, "Why Men Still Can't Have It All," *Esquire*, June/July 2013; P. Mountford, "I'm Not a Hero for Taking Care of My Kids," *Slate*, July 10, 2013; J. A. Smith, *The Daddy Shift: How Stay-at-Home Dads, Breadwinning Moms, and Shared Parenting Are Transforming the American Family* (Boston: Beacon Press, 2009); J. A. Smith, "Five Reasons Why It's a Good Time to Be a Dad," *Greater Good* (UC Berkeley), June 12, 2013, at http://greatergood.berkeley.edu/article/item/five_reasons_why_its_a_good_time_to_be_a_dad; C. P. Williams, "Fatherhood, Manhood, and Having It All," *The Daily Beast*, June 28, 2013, at http://www.thedailybeast.com/witw/articles/2013/06/28/fatherhood-manhood-and-having-it-all.html.

72 There are infinite possibilities. See S. D. Friedman, *Total Leadership: Be a Better Leader, Have a Richer Life* (Boston, MA: Harvard Business Review Press, 2008).

73 S. Meers and J. Strober, *Getting to 50/50: How Working Couples Can Have It All* (Berkeley, CA: Viva Editions, 2013).

74 See, for just a few examples, Gerson, *The Unfinished Revolution*; C. Rivers and R. C. Barnett, *The New Soft War on Women: How the Myth of Female Ascendance Is Hurting Women, Men—and Our Economy* (New York: Penguin, 2013); and S. Coontz, "Why Gender Equality Stalled," *New York Times*, February 16, 2013.

Index

About the Author

Stewart D. Friedman is an organizational psychologist at the Wharton School of the University of Pennsylvania, where he has been on the faculty since 1984 and emeritus since 2019. He worked for five years in the mental health field before earning his PhD from the University of Michigan. In 1991, as founding director of the Wharton Leadership Program (now called the McNulty Leadership Program), he initiated the school's core leadership courses, including the Learning Teams. A few years later, he launched the Leadership Fellows. More recently, he cofounded Wharton's P3: Purpose, Passion, Principles—a cocurricular experience run collaboratively by students, faculty, and administrators. He also founded Wharton's Work/Life Integration Project in 1991.

Friedman has been recognized by the biennial Thinkers50 global ranking of management thinkers repeatedly since 2011. He was honored with its 2015 Distinguished Achievement Award as the world's number one expert in talent management and was inducted into its Hall of Fame in 2023. He was listed among *HR Magazine*'s most influential thought leaders, chosen by *Working Mother* as one of America's most influential men who have made life better for working parents, and presented with the Families and Work Institute's Work Life Legacy Award.

While on leave from Wharton for two and a half years, Friedman ran a 50-person department as the senior executive for leadership development at Ford Motor Company. In partnership with the CEO, he launched a corporate-wide portfolio of initiatives designed to transform Ford's culture; 2,500-plus managers per year participated. Near the end of his tenure at Ford, an independent research group (ICEDR) said the Leadership Development Center was a "global benchmark" for companies striving to accelerate the growth of their people. At Ford, he created Total Leadership, which has been a popular Wharton course since 2001 and is used by individuals and companies worldwide, including as a primary intervention in a multiyear study funded by the National Institutes of Health on improving the careers and lives of women in medicine and by 135,000-plus students in Friedman's first massive open online course (MOOC) on Coursera. Participants in this program complete an intensive series of challenging exercises that increase their leadership capacity, performance, and well-being in all parts of life, while working in peer-to-peer coaching relationships.

His research is widely cited, including among *Harvard Business Review*'s "Ideas That Shaped Management," and he has written two bestselling books, *Total Leadership: Be a Better Leader, Have a Richer Life* (2008) and *Leading the Life You Want: Skills for Integrating Work and Life* (2014). In 2013, Wharton School Press published his landmark study of two generations of Wharton students, *Baby Bust: New Choices for Men and Women in Work and Family*. *Work and Family—Allies or Enemies?* (2000) was recognized by the *Wall Street Journal* as one of the field's best books. In *Integrating Work and Life: The Wharton Resource Guide* (1998), Friedman edited the first collection of learning tools for building leadership skills for integrating work and life. His latest book is *Parents Who Lead: The Leadership Approach You Need to Parent with Purpose, Fuel Your Career, and Create a Richer Life* (2020).

Winner of many teaching awards, he appears regularly in business media (the *New York Times* cited the "rock star adoration" he inspires in his students). Friedman serves on a number of boards and is an in-demand speaker, consultant, coach, workshop leader, public policy adviser (to the U.S. Departments of Labor and State, the United Nations, and two White House administrations), and advocate for family-supportive policies in the private sector. Follow him on Twitter @StewFriedman and LinkedIn, read his 50-plus digital articles on HBR.org, and tune in to his podcast *Work and Life with Stew Friedman* (since 2014).

About Wharton School Press

Wharton School Press, the book publishing arm of the Wharton School of the University of Pennsylvania, was established to inspire bold, insightful thinking within the global business community.

An imprint of University of Pennsylvania Press, Wharton School Press publishes a select list of award-winning, bestselling, and thought-leading books that offer trusted business knowledge to help leaders at all levels meet the challenges of today and the opportunities of tomorrow. Led by a spirit of innovation and experimentation, Wharton School Press leverages groundbreaking digital technologies and has pioneered a fast-reading business book format that fits readers' busy lives, allowing them to swiftly emerge with the tools and information needed to make an impact. Wharton School Press books offer guidance and inspiration on a variety of topics, including leadership, management, strategy, innovation, entrepreneurship, finance, marketing, social impact, public policy, and more.

To find books that will inspire and empower you to increase your impact and expand your personal and professional horizons, visit wsp.wharton.upenn.edu.

About The Wharton School

Founded in 1881 as the world's first collegiate business school, the Wharton School of the University of Pennsylvania is shaping the future of business by incubating ideas, driving insights, and creating leaders who change the world. With a faculty of more than 235 renowned professors, Wharton has 5,000 undergraduate, MBA, executive MBA, and doctoral students. Each year 13,000 professionals from around the world advance their careers through Wharton Executive Education's individual, company-customized, and online programs. More than 100,000 Wharton alumni form a powerful global network of leaders who transform business every day.

www.wharton.upenn.edu

UNIVERSITY OF
PENNSYLVANIA
PRESS

About Penn Press

True to its Philadelphia roots, Penn Press is well known for its distinguished list of publications in American history and culture, including innovative work on the transnational currents that surrounded and shaped the republic from the colonial period through the present, as well as prize-winning publications in urban studies. The Press is equally renowned for its publications in European history, literature, and culture from late antiquity through the early modern period. Penn Press's social science publications tackle contemporary political issues of concern to a broad readership of citizens and scholars, notably including a long-standing commitment to publishing path-breaking work in international human rights. Penn Press also publishes outstanding works in archaeology, economic history, business, and Jewish Studies in partnership with local institutions.

You can learn more about our recent publications by visiting www.pennpress.org or viewing our seasonal catalogs.

Printed in the USA
CPSIA information can be obtained
at www.ICGtesting.com
JSHW020518211223
54019JS00006B/9